DEMYSTIFYING
PERFORMANCE
MANAGEMENT

PUBLISHED BY AVOCET BOOKS
www.avocetbooks.com

ISBN:

eBook	978-1-963678-09-3
Hardcover	978-1-963678-17-8
Paperback	978-1-963678-10-9

First Edition

BOOK PRODUCTION BY HAL CLIFFORD ASSOCIATES
www.hcabooks.com

DEMYSTIFYING PERFORMANCE MANAGEMENT: GETTING MORE THINGS DONE THE RIGHT WAY

The Complete Guide for Achieving Superior Performance Now

PAUL MBITHI

Dedication

I dedicate this book to the memory of my father, Joseph M. Mbithi, for instilling in me the values of hard work and loyalty and for inspiring me to demand excellence of myself and to serve others; and to my son, Joseph Mbithi Jr., for the joy he brings in my everyday life.

TABLE OF CONTENTS

About This Book

I wrote this book to share lessons on things that I have learnt in my career about performance management and using these skills to make things work better. I have noticed that in spite of many training and other information-sharing sessions, managers still struggle with the topic of performance management, and employees still feel that their contributions to their organisations are not adequately recognised and appreciated. Speaking to managers and employee groups helped me realise that there is need for a "how-to" type of book that guides individuals, managers, executives and entire organisations throughout the performance management cycle and its related events and activities. As an organisation goes through the activities described in this book, the reader can pick up the book at the relevant chapter and see how he can apply some of the ideas to make the work less painful and more fulfilling for all involved. If I have managed to achieve this need then I am grateful to the Almighty. If there are any flaws in argument or reasoning then those should be attributed to me.

Acknowledgments

I thank my family for believing in me. I thank God for his numerous gifts.

I have drawn a lot of lessons and ideas from interacting with a number of people. I am grateful to the individuals and teams that I have worked with. I have had the opportunity to successfully implement many of the ideas in this book. I am grateful to the clients who have provided me with the opportunity to work with them on performance management projects. Client confidentiality prevents me from mentioning specific names, but you know yourselves and I am forever grateful.

INTRODUCTION

A T BERNARD'S ACCOUNTING THERE WERE two things that were certain—employees would be very busy and overworked during the year, and employees would leave in droves after the annual performance reviews. The latter is not only a problem at Bernard's Accounting or at similar companies, but it is a challenge that is prevalent in many organisations. Employees are disgruntled with the outcomes of performance management processes. This disenchantment stems from a number of factors emanating from the employees, their supervisors and management in general. Employees, for their part, have little or no say on their performance objectives, and they tend to take a wait-and-see stance on the fulfilment of set objectives. Supervisors are not rigorous or consistent in the promotion of performance management practices, and management tends to ignore promises or initiatives designed to support employee development. These employee development programs are usually not honoured due to busy schedules and failure to prioritise them. On the other hand, managers are also busy doing other things which ostensibly seem to be given more importance than employee development and performance alignment. The result of this is that at the end of the performance period, which is usually annual, the manager does not have enough information to render a holistic, unbiased and objective evaluation of the employee's performance during the entire year. The employee feels sidelined and treated unfairly, and he starts plotting his next move outside the current organisation.

I have written this book to guide managers and executives in this important subject so that they may effectively carry out the activities that comprise performance management. I have also witnessed a number of cases in which individuals are promoted and assigned responsibilities to oversee a group of people. These new managers have not been schooled in the techniques and practices of performance management, and as such they find themselves avoiding those tasks related to performance management or even giving them inadequate time and attention. The end result is that neither the manager nor the employee goes beyond the rubrics of checking and confirming whether goals were achieved, overlooking a number of important aspects such as the intrinsic development of the individuals that a manager supervises. In the chapter about the rigour of the performance management system, I discuss a number of elements which the newly promoted manager should thoroughly familiarise himself with and which executives should coach their upcoming leaders on.

Earlier in my consulting career I developed an interest in performance management because it formed a link between strategy and execution by providing managers with tools to plan employee tasks and goals based on the individual capability and interest and based on the organisational needs. I was working with a large bank, and the assignment required us to review its performance management practices and propose recommendations. I sat down with my colleague and developed a list of questions that covered the entire performance management cycle as we conceived it then and used this to gauge the extent to which the different elements were practiced in that bank.

The tool proved to be useful as it allowed us to uncover the different viewpoints of employees based on whether they were management or non-management staff, newly employed or long-serving employees, and the functional areas that they represented. It led me to the conclusion that in that bank there was no single shared view about what performance management is nor about its importance. This led to inconsistency in the related management practices. I decided to venture deeper into the subject to find out if this was an exception. In the thirty projects that I undertook after this, my conclusion remained the same. I wondered whether this had to do with leadership or with the occupants of the human resource office. In 2018, I developed a Performance Management Training program which I have offered to over one thousand individuals either in full or in part. In its first edition I trained more than one hundred senior managers of a commercial bank, and the feedback I received was once again indicative of the need to streamline performance management practices and even to provide similar frameworks to be used throughout the bank.

I have also received feedback on the content and topics from the individuals and organisations that I have trained. The program is centred on the business value of performance management practices and ensuring that each element and practice resonates with business users, especially executives. I have reviewed performance management systems for more than twenty organisations, both for-profit and not-for-profit entities. My reviews have led to the development of the content of this book as they have provided me with the raw material. I have also supported organisations in my consultancy career in reviewing their performance management systems with the goal of improving them, and this led me to develop a number of frameworks, tools and checklists, some of which I describe and discuss in this book.

What Performance Management Is

How to make employees perform consistently at all times is the key focus of this book. I believe that it is no longer tenable to manage an informed workforce through threats and coercion as these might have short-term gains but result in long-term challenges. Performance management refers to those activities undertaken by organisations to align the goals of employees with those of the organisation in order to achieve planned financial and other results. Performance management, therefore, should be seen as an ongoing process with a number of defining moments that can either enhance or dilute employee experience. The employee experience has a direct correlation to customer experience and thus to strategy success.

Bernard's Accounting, described earlier, had a peculiar performance appraisal period. Managers in this company only bothered about performance management when it was time for performance appraisal, and at that time the reviews were done hurriedly, lacked backup information and were often one-sided. Employees would argue that they were not aware of some of the issues that were raised by their managers during the appraisal process and even more so about how these issues were used against them to lower their final performance rating or score. Employees also argued that there was no evidence either way that what was required of them during the year in question had been tracked or reported on. This led to mass employee exoduses after the annual appraisal period. The company could not retain the core workforce which it required to serve its large clientele.

What then was missing in the practice of performance management at Bernard's Accounting? Why were the outcomes of the performance appraisal process often disputed? *Performance management* is a systematic and planned set of activities for managing the behaviour of people within a context that facilitates and supports the alignment of individual goals with organisational goals in order to achieve the organisation's strategy. *Performance appraisals*, on the other hand, are tools for measuring the extent to which an employee met planned objectives. They are tools used to assess how efficient employees are in delivering against their job responsibilities. Many organisations tend to assume that performance management and performance appraisals are essentially the same thing. This is inaccurate. While performance appraisals can be a subset or an element of a well-functioning performance management system, it is perfectly possible to have a performance management system that does not include performance appraisals. Performance management has a broader impact than simply assessing the extent to which an employee met planned objectives. It focuses on the totality of the employee to ensure that the work being carried out, how it is managed, resources and relationships required, and the organisational environment are all synchronised in such a way that both the organisation and the employee benefit. This synchronicity was lacking at Bernard's Accounting LLP.

Performance management systems come into play in making an effort to harness and coordinate individual efforts towards the attainment of overall goals. Organisations invest a lot of time and resources in crafting their strategies so as to have road maps to follow in pursuit of their goals. There are a number of tools and actors that are brought into the strategy-setting process. At times external consultants are invited to facilitate strategy discussions because of the importance that the organisation places in getting it right when it comes to strategy. The strategy is usually cascaded to the organisational units and departments so that it can be relevant to all parts of the organisation. The cascaded strategy is then further broken down into initiatives and activities so that individuals can be clear on what is expected of them in the pursuit of organisational goals. The strategy may be developed to cover a number of years; however, some organisations are beginning to adopt shorter strategic-planning horizons based on the rapid changes that are taking place in the internal and external environments. This cascading process and translating of general strategic themes into measurable objectives is the first and key activity of any performance management system.

Performance management systems come into play in making an effort to harness and coordinate individual efforts towards the attainment of overall goals. Managers may at times know what the strategy requires but find it difficult to translate into measurable, lower-level objectives that are carried out amid the pressing demands of operational activities, which tend to take most of employees' working hours.

Performance management is about planning, delivering and monitoring business results according to an organisation's strategy—so strategy drives performance just as performance drives strategy. An effective performance management system should therefore be aligned to the organisation's strategy by putting in place the required tools, systems and processes required to operationalise the strategy. One of these tools is the performance appraisal.

There is no perfect performance appraisal method. In organisations, performance appraisals are conducted for a variety of administrative purposes such as salary recommendations, promotion and layoff decisions and developmental purposes such as training recommendations. The goals associated with administrative and developmental appraisals can conflict with one another, and even when the goals are reasonably compatible, one performance appraisal method is unlikely to be the best match for every purpose. Throughout the book, I provide some scenarios of organisational performance management practices, which show the reader what others are doing, so as to benefit from what works and avoid what does not. A practice gaining currency is an organisation's separating of the administrative and reward management dimensions of performance appraisals.

Performance management is, therefore, a management practice of developing a link between individual and organisational performance in the interest of the organisation's vision and mission. Performance appraisals for their part are a way of measuring how effectively an employee supports the organisation in achieving its mission. In between the performance-planning process and the performance appraisal activity are a number of elements and practices that form part of performance management.

This book provides the manager with a number of tools to be used in any workplace, whether large or small, to bring out the creative juices of the individuals and groups as well as to provide structure and consistency in the performance management process. Organisations spend millions of dollars on facilities, equipment, information and communication systems so that their people can do the work necessary to stay in business. Yet they overlook the importance of planning and evaluating the functionality of standards and work rules and the contributions of performance support tools to help people learn their jobs more quickly and perform to the set standard more consistently. The manager's and supervisor's role is to give the appropriate people feedback on the functionality of the workspace, equipment and systems. They must also help evaluate the usefulness of and advocate for the availability and improvement of job aids or quick-reference guides, job templates, standards, and work rules and procedures.

Managers are encouraged to involve their staff in the planning, monitoring and reviewing steps so as to gain acceptability and congruence in performance-related decisions. The workplace standards and expectations are crafted by management, and they expect the employees to adopt these standards and live accordingly. These standards and expectations must be reviewed periodically and not annually, as once per year is too infrequent to make required changes.

Poor Performance Management Is Costly

FourUp Explore is a mining company that had a showroom to provide visibility of the company's products. The showroom supervisor was responsible for growing sales and ensuring proper recordkeeping of the showroom operations. When I visited this showroom, I wondered why the organisation did not achieve its financial targets and whether the performance management system was fully aligned to the organisation's workings. One of the things I found out is that the performance expectations were not shared and accepted by the showroom staff. Management expected them to produce $1 million in sales every year, while the showroom staff had set themselves a target of $400,000. Additionally, the reporting system was not well built, and the interface between the invoicing process and the accounting system was not real-time—meaning that sales were not captured in the accounting system on time, and the staff rewards were delayed as a result. The misalignment between employee expectations and company expectations was clear. There was also inadequacy in the systems and processes that were supposed to enable employees to deliver the expected results.

The cost of labour has continued to increase, and organisations are keen to see their return on investment. The notion of human beings as a resource similar to machinery and equipment has somewhat changed because humans have become the key resource. It has therefore become important to adopt different practices to improve and align the employee's performance to that of the organisation. The recent COVID-19 pandemic saw an increase in the value given to the human being and to employee experience touchpoints. Employee experience touchpoints are points of contact between a company and its employees that can influence an employee's perception of the company. A number of these touchpoints relate to the performance management cycle and its various outputs. Adopting cost-effective ways of managing staff is thus not only an HR imperative but one that spans the entire organisation. In Chapter 6, "The Rigour of Measuring and Monitoring Performance," I explain why in some jobs budget performance is an indicator of success, while in Chapter 1, "The Purpose of Performance Management," I discuss different philosophical approaches about leveraging on the productivity of employees. In a later chapter on the management of key performance indicators, I explain the need of financial KPIs that are aligned to the organisation's strategy.

Additionally, the mass customisation of jobs and the rising involvement of multiple stakeholders in the performance management process suggest that a number of things need to change if organisations are going to get the best out of their most critical resource—their people. The development and alignment of employee competencies to meet stakeholder expectations is one of these areas. Coupled with this, the acceleration of the gig economy and introduction of the workplace together demand that employees constantly demonstrate superior performance lest they be replaced. How to make employees perform consistently at all times is the key focus of this book. It is no longer tenable to manage an informed workforce through threats and coercion, as these might have short-term gains but result in long-term challenges. Performance management, therefore, should be seen as an ongoing process with a number of defining moments that enhance or dilute employee experience. The employee experience has a direct correlation to customer experience and thus to strategy success. This creates a positive employee experience largely through the motivational effect of carefully worded and constructive feedback, as well as the feeling of undertaking purposeful work.

Change Requires Performance Management

Today's world requires managers to be keen on the performance of their staff and also to be focused on delivering business results. This has always been the case, but there are a number of variables that have changed and that keep changing. These changing variables require managers to refresh and rethink their practices on people management. The globalisation of labour, which started over a decade ago, means that labour mobility has increased and employers are able to obtain skills from a number of countries if the laws allow. Flexible labour is also available to meet an organisation's short-term manpower needs. The global talent pool is more accessible to organisations than ever before. This phenomenon means that when employees do not perform at the required level they are easily replaceable, in theory, by other, more willing or capable employees. But this is likely to create a negative trend and increase business costs related to the recruitment and onboarding of staff. It is therefore imperative that managers instill superior performance practices in their employees rather than seeking to replace them if they are not as productive as expected. The war for talent continues unabated, and employees will move to organisations where they feel they will be better handled or even recognised for their efforts at delivering business results.

From a performance-improvement perspective, facilities, equipment, tools and the like are essential; however, some things should be done for each of them to live up to expectations. FourUp Explore had invested in stonecutting machinery, which, at the time I worked with them, was already obsolete; the housing of the machinery was ineffective as it did not provide ergonomically sound working conditions for the technical staff. Such a consideration—while most managers would not address it—has a big impact on how well employees meet their performance objectives and is often what employees attribute failure to in the likely event of failure occurring. Workspace and layout, for example, should be designed to support the requirements of the job, not be entitlements for seniority or position status. This means someone should be responsible for studying how work is done to identify the behaviours the space is expected to support. Equipment should have the functionality required to support the tasks people perform. This means someone should be responsible for confirming what is required in order to complete the tasks and that the equipment has the expected functions. The role of the line manager has expanded a lot over the years, and there is need to integrate cross-functional roles such that employee performance experience is not compromised due to a failure in a related component of the overall organisational system.

Good Performance Management Can Reduce Turnover

The rise in Generation Y also brings a number of performance challenges. Generation Y has been typified as being impatient, and many have admitted changing jobs as many as four times a year, the economy permitting.

Organisational goals are mostly long-term, and if an organisation cannot rely on employees to be devoted to seeing these goals achieved due to high labour mobility, a problem arises which performance management must address for this category of staff. Increasingly, organisations are also adopting shorter strategic-planning cycles, in which results need to be demonstrated within months if not weeks. The pressure to perform has intensified.

In Chapter 1, "Purpose of Performance Management," I discuss why and how the performance management system is linked to strategy. Strategy by its very nature has both an internal and external focus. The organisation's strategy therefore has to recognise the external happenings that have an impact on performance and productivity, and managers have to align their style to that reality. At the time of writing this book, debates on the impact of Generation Z in the organisation have begun. The needs of real human beings should be the focus of both strategy and performance management.

The goal-setting process starts from the strategy and uses information obtained from a number of internal and external sources so as to have a coherent way of planning the contribution of individuals to the attainment of organisational goals. Goals tend to be long term in nature and are broken down into objectives, which in turn are broken down into plans and activities for implementation. The goals are documented in a system for periodic reference and update. The parameters and sources on which the goals are set often change, and it is upon the manager to take note of these changes in order to align the goals to the changed reality. Strategy is not static, even though it is developed for a three-to-five-year horizon. Emergent strategy takes into account the changes and opportunities in the environment so as to further the interests of the organisation in pursuit of its mission and vision. Some of the emergent issues could relate to the internal environment, where for example, performance may be impaired by malfunctioning infrastructure or unavailability of the required tools and support.

One of the biggest challenges managers and supervisors face is how to bring people up to speed as quickly as possible. Some organisations spend years training people to do their jobs. Other organisations try to hire people with some degree of readiness; however, all organisations find they must share in the responsibility for helping people become proficient as quickly as possible. People are proficient when they can do a job or task consistently to an acceptable level under normal circumstances. The role of managers and supervisors in equipping people for the job is in areas of orientation, readiness assessments, formal trainings, and on-the-job trainings. Mastery of this skill by managers is bound to result in spectacular business performance and outcomes. In addition, Massive Open Online Courses (MOOCs) are available to managers in the process of developing their employees' skills and capability.

Bad Performance Management Can Cause Problems

No matter how experienced, managers and supervisors are susceptible to a number of rater errors. Some raters are "easy graders" and give all employees, regardless of their actual performance, scores at the high end of the performance-rating scale. Other raters tend to be "hard graders" and give all employees scores at the low end of the performance-rating scale. Still others tend to give scores that cluster at the scale midpoint. These errors are problematic because they misrepresent the actual range and distribution of employee performance. Self-awareness of one's management style and tendencies is a skill that a manager needs to acquire. Managers should also be open to feedback from their employees and from their peers in order to adjust their styles and to avoid subjectivity and bias in the performance appraisal process and the overall performance management activities.

Performance appraisal methods can be organised into four basic types: 1) those that assess the employee's personal characteristics, 2) those that rate the employee's work behaviour, 3) those that rate the employee's work results, and 4) those that rate an employee's overall value or worth in comparison to other employees. Each of these methods has its own advantages and disadvantages; however, organisations at times develop instruments that unsuccessfully attempt to merge all these systems in a way that lacks coherence and cohesion. In Chapter 6, "The Rigour of Measuring and Monitoring Performance," I discuss various ways to avoid rater errors and how to harness the power of integrated feedback mechanisms. Senior management in many organisations intervenes through a process of performance moderation to also address the issue of rater bias and to ensure that individual and departmental performance is aligned to the organisation's performance. This intervention should consider documented performance records and trends as well as the portfolio of evidence in the employees' possession.

Most employees think that performance management is about performance appraisals, and they gear all their efforts towards achieving the goals agreed in their performance contracts. This limited view of performance management that equates it with performance appraisal is based largely on the fact that rewards and career-growth prospects are linked to performance appraisals. Other elements of performance management, such as fostering employee growth and motivation, seem to be largely left out, and a lot of work and time is spent discussing whether or not employees have met performance goals.

You might be wondering if the practices described in this book are applicable to all kinds of organisations irrespective of size and industry. Just like management is context-specific, these pieces of advice are intended to be applied based on the organisational context. A nonprofit organisation can and should have a strategy; however, the financial objectives it pursues would relate to sustainability and the ability to draw resources from a variety of sources. It would still require key performance indicators, but the naming conventions used and the focus of these indicators would differ from the way they would be used in a business entity. A small organisation that employs a handful of individuals would benefit from the practices of monitoring and measuring performance even if these activities would be carried out using less sophisticated means—because the goal is not to use sophisticated measurement tools but rather to measure achievement of the set objectives that are aligned to the strategy.

Organisations these days are categorical that they reward results and not efforts. The efforts that employees put into their work and into carrying out the duties for which they are employed play a part in achieving the set goals. That said, managers should direct employee efforts in such a way that they feel their contribution is being valued and recognised. Those activities or actions that call for reward or recognition should be clearly spelt out, and so should their associated rewards. It is not enough to have a set of unattainable rewards that do not fall within the range of employees' actions. A rewards policy, no matter how simple, should be part and parcel of the tools implemented to coordinate and direct employee efforts towards success. The rewards policy should be customised to meet the unique needs of the workforce. A tool that organisations can use to achieve this end is described in Chapter 8, "Activities to Reward and Recognise Performance."

The performance management system should be designed to meet the organisation's goals and objectives. In order to do this, the performance management system requires a framework. A framework is a way of integrating performance management practices into a consistent whole. Everything needs to be tied together and linked so that activities are not carried out in an isolated fashion. A successful framework for a certain organisation might not work in your company; thus, it is important to ensure that the framework employed is suited to your organisational culture, strategy and operating environment. In order to ensure completeness in the performance management system, a framework provides you with key areas of focus. One such framework is the *Plan, Perform and Improve* framework. This framework starts with strategy and goals in the "Plan" step, then focuses on getting strategy executed in the "Perform" step and finally putting in place improvements for the next performance period. The framework, however, does not include the developmental and other activities carried out during the performance period, assuming that managers will carry them out all the same.

High-Performance Culture

A *high-performance culture* is an organisational environment in which individuals and groups are geared to consistently achieving high business results. It is not a matter of complying to the performance management calendar or to the elements of the performance management cycle. It is about using all these tools and frameworks to consistently achieve superior results and create wins for the employees, the departments, the organisation, its stakeholders and customers at large. High-performing organisations outperform their competitors in a number of areas as they put in deliberate efforts to address performance issues and concerns as they arise. They also reinforce the superior practices which make them stand out in the eyes of customers and other constituents by ensuring that employee behaviours and standards are geared towards fulfilling the organisation's strategic objectives in alignment with the customer expectations and the environmental dictates.

It is my intention that in reading this book managers and executives will identify behavioural and structural elements which they will adapt in their organisation based on its respective nuances in order to create a high-performance culture. A high-performance culture helps the organisation achieve high levels of performance and results consistently over time. It does this intentionally, mostly through the leadership actions that are intentionally designed to drive congruent behaviour. The activities and processes described in this book therefore cannot be taken as events and carried out once. They must be made to stick and be part of the organisation's very essence. An executive who speaks about equity and fairness and then goes ahead to promote individuals who do not espouse the organisational values is setting a bad precedent and damaging the culture.

Building a high-performance culture should, therefore, be the goal of every executive and manager. A high-performance culture can signify the difference between stagnation and growth, competitiveness and leading the competition. It does not matter whether you work in a nonprofit organisation or a business entity—your organisation will benefit greatly by putting in place the ingredients required for a high-performing culture because achieving results is sector independent.

The PERFORMANCE Framework

In order to ensure a comprehensive system is used, I propose the *12-Dimension PERFORMANCE framework*. This framework uses the initials of the word *performance* to focus managers and other executives' attention on what they should aim to achieve through the implementation of a robust performance management system. It does this by posing key questions within each dimension of the framework. The framework can be used by organisations who are developing a new performance management system or who would like to update or review their current one. The framework can also be used by managers and employers to ensure that they drive performance in their organisations and achieve a performance culture. A description of these alternative uses is contained in the sections that follow. The table below defines each of the elements of the PERFORMANCE framework and points out the key questions that are posed in each area. It is not a static framework, and users can add additional considerations that are aligned to the dimension definitions.

Table 1 : Performance Management Framework

DIMENSION	DEFINITION	KEY QUESTIONS
P PURPOSE	This dimension explores the need for a performance management system and what it seeks to achieve in the organisation.	• Why do you have a performance management system? • Is it for promotion, rewards or employee development? • Is the purpose of the performance management system aligned to the organisational purpose?
E EMPLOYEE	This dimension describes the role of the employee within the performance management system and cycle. The employee is anyone employed by an organisation to develop, deliver or oversee the production of goods and services.	• What is the role of the employee in the performance management system? • What training will employees require to adopt the system adequately? • Which employee populations will the system cover? • Is the performance management system a means of employee engagement?

DIMENSION	DEFINITION	KEY QUESTIONS
R **REVIEWS**	This dimension relates to the aspect of performance management that covers the formal appraisal or evaluation processes.	• How often will reviews be carried out? • Who will carry out the reviews and how will the information be obtained? • What is the content of the reviews? • How will objectivity in reviews be enhanced?
F **FORMAT**	This dimension describes the formal aspect of performance management which is normally documented in a number of ways.	• What format will the performance appraisal instrument take? • What rating scales will be used? • What tools will be used to document various elements of the performance management system? • Will they be automated, semi-automated or manual?
O **OPENNESS**	This dimension is about the degree to which the performance management system and its outputs will be open or closed.	• To what extent will the performance management system be open and allow input from external sources? • Who will have access to the information contained in the performance management system?
R **RIGOUR**	This area covers the thoroughness or amount of effort required in administering the performance management system and its elements.	• What level of rigour is required in using the system? Basic? Intermediate? Advanced? • What content will be covered? Behaviours? Values? Strategy?

DIMENSION	DEFINITION	KEY QUESTIONS
M **MANAGEMENT**	The management dimension deals with the role of management in the system. Management here is anyone who achieves results through others.	• What is the role of management in the performance management system? • How often will they be involved and how is their involvement captured?
A **ACTIVITIES**	The activities dimension details all the activities, their sequencing and timing throughout the performance management cycle.	• What performance management system activities are envisaged? Coaching sessions? Update meetings? Review sessions? • Which activities will managers carry out, and which ones will staff carry out? • Which activities can be customised or personalised to meet the unique needs of employees?
N **NUANCES**	This dimension reveals the unique organisational attributes that need to be considered throughout the performance life cycle.	• What is unique in this organisation, which cannot be replicated? • What are the unique and special attributes in a given organisation, including the size and complexity, role of HR, maturity of HR? • How will the system reflect the organisational culture and values?
C **CONVENIENCE**	This dimension looks at the ways of enhancing the elements of performance management to make them more convenient.	• How can the goal-cascade process be simplified? • Are tools simple to use? Do the tools have instructions and tips?

DIMENSION	DEFINITION	KEY QUESTIONS
E **ENVIRONMENT**	This dimension looks at the stability or otherwise of the practices governed by the system and the manner in which interventions can be incorporated to deal with flux.	• Is the environment changing or stable, and how will this be reflected in the system and tool design? • How does the organisation alter performance management measures in line with the changes in the environment?

You will notice that from the above framework there are a number of elements that are not static. Not least is the environment in which most organisations operate.

This framework of viewing the performance management dimensions also works as a useful tool for managers to hold discussions around the performance management system, especially with new employees and even to refresh the knowledge of existing employees. The manager can either pose questions to the employee to gauge his level of understanding of the different components or walk through each dimension and provide explanations or clarifications.

An example of how the manager-driven use of the 12-Dimension framework can be carried out is illustrated below:

**Table 2: Manager use of the 12-Dimension
Performance Management System framework**

P **PURPOSE**	• Manager to Employee: Do you understand the purpose of our performance management system?
E **EMPLOYEE**	• Manager to Employee: Are you familiar with the company performance management policy?
R **REVIEWS**	• Manager to Employee: Your performance will be formally assessed two times a year, and other informal reviews will take place twice a quarter. Do you understand how this will be carried out and the subject of discussion?

F	**FORMAT**	• Manager to Employee: Have you gone through the performance appraisal form, its sections and rating scales, and are there sections you would like to discuss?
O	**OPENNESS**	• Manager to Employee: The outcome of your performance evaluation will be made known to senior leadership, the HR department and other departmental managers. Are you aware and comfortable about that?
R	**RIGOUR**	• Manager to Employee: You will be assessed on your ability to meet business requirements, ethical business practice and demonstrating behaviours at the right level as defined in the competencies found in the handbook. Are you familiar with your performance expectations?
M	**MANAGEMENT**	• Manager to Employee: To help you meet your performance objectives, management will track results and outcomes and develop interventions to support goal achievement and your development.
A	**ACTIVITIES**	• Manager to Employee: We will carry out a number of activities to recognise good performers. Would you like to discuss the activities that you will be required to carry out over the performance period? What activities did you carry out over the performance period in comparison to what was planned?
N	**NUANCES**	• Manager to Employee: We value innovation and accountability in this organisation, and you will be rewarded for bringing in innovative ideas and stepping outside your comfort zone. What do you think you can do in your current role?
C	**CONVENIENCE**	• Manager to Employee: How can we make this system and formats easier for you to use consistently? What changes do you need to make in your work schedule to accommodate the performance management activities?
E	**ENVIRONMENT**	• Manager to Employee: If the assumptions on which our strategy is based change, we will review your goals and objectives and make adjustments accordingly.

The 12-Dimension framework can also be used by employees to initiate dialogue with their line managers on the various elements of the performance management system. The typical way employees do this is by asking questions to their manager. These questions lead to engagement and foster alignment between employee and manager expectations.

An illustration of the employee-driven dialogue along the framework is illustrated below:

Table 3 : Employee-Driven Dialogue around the 12-Dimension performance management system Framework

P	**PURPOSE**	• *Employee:* Why do we have/need a performance management system? • *Manager:* The purpose of our performance management system is to develop good performers to grow and to achieve our strategic goals
E	**EMPLOYEE**	• *Employee:* What do I need to do in order to be rewarded for good performance? • *Manager:* As an employee you will be required to familiarise yourself with the performance management policy and comply with it.
R	**REVIEWS**	• *Employee:* How often will my performance be reviewed? • *Employee:* Who will review my performance and what information will be used? • *Manager:* I will formally assess your performance twice a year as your line manager. I will base my assessment on the objectives and goals we agree on at the beginning of the year. • *Manager:* I will obtain inputs from customers, your peers and those who report to you.

F	**FORMAT**	• *Employee:* What rating scales will be used to assess my performance? • *Employee:* Is there any form that I need to complete in order to document my performance? And where can I obtain it? • *Employee:* Where do I store the completed self-assessments? • *Manager:* The organisation uses a performance appraisal form which can be found on the intranet, and you will be rated using alphabetic letters A, B, C, and D, where A is excellent performance and D is unsatisfactory performance. • *Manager:* You will carry out a self-rating in the online form and submit it electronically for my further review. • *Manager:* Completed appraisal forms can be viewed in the system or downloaded onto your computer.
O	**OPENNESS**	• *Employee:* Will other employees have access to my performance reviews? • *Employee:* Who will have access to the information contained in the performance management system? • *Manager:* The outcome of your performance evaluation will be made known only to senior leadership, the HR department and other departmental managers. For purposes of rewards management, compliance and disciplinary matters, your reviews may be made accessible to other parties as described in the performance handbook.
R	**RIGOUR**	• *Employee:* Is it easy to receive an overall rating of A? • *Employee:* How difficult is it to use the information in the handbook? • *Employee:* Will my performance be based only on the achievement of sales targets? • *Manager:* There are cases where employees receive a high overall rating based on demonstrating the agreed behaviours and achieving the desired results. You will be assessed on your ability to meet business requirements, ethical business practice and demonstrating behaviours at the right level as defined in the competencies found in the handbook. This information will be updated periodically in the system.

M MANAGEMENT

- *Employee:* What is the role of other managers with whom I work in determining my final rating?
- *Employee:* Can I choose which manager or projects I want to work with?
- *Manager:* Other managers with whom you have worked will contribute to your final rating. The choice of work is dependent on your job description and management's decisions.

A ACTIVITIES

- *Employee:* Apart from the two formal reviews, what other performance management activities will I be expected to carry out?
- *Employee:* What support can I expect to receive from you to improve my performance?
- *Manager:* You will be provided with a Performance Management handbook, which describes our performance calendar. In addition to the two formal reviews, we will have monthly informal review sessions in which we will discuss your performance, challenges faced and support required. It is your duty to schedule these informal monthly meetings.
- *Manager:* You will receive timely performance feedback, on-the-job coaching, training and any other needed support in order to improve your performance.

N NUANCES

- *Employee:* Are there any other specific guidelines that you would like to provide to me? Things to look out for or things to avoid?
- *Manager:* We value innovation and accountability in this organisation, and you will be rewarded for bringing in innovative ideas and stepping outside your comfort zone.

C CONVENIENCE

- *Employee:* Can we have performance discussions outside the formal timetable?
- *Manager:* It is advisable to not only have performance discussions during the formal evaluation periods but throughout the year.

E	**ENVIRONMENT**	• *Employee:* What happens if I am not able to sell enough widgets because of factors outside my control? • *Manager:* If the assumptions on which our strategy is based change, we will review your goals and objectives and make adjustments accordingly. It is your responsibility to communicate these changes in a timely manner.

The remaining chapters of this book are dedicated to each of the elements of the PERFORMANCE framework.

This book provides anyone involved in managing performance with guidance, tools and ideas on how to improve the current performance practices in the organisation. It goes beyond the performance appraisal tools and processes by providing a holistic year-round view of performance management and performance improvement. It further responds to thought-provoking questions, which any modern manager needs to answer. Productivity tips on how to manage the expectations of stakeholders while still achieving one's own mandate have been included. The alignment of employee performance to the needs and expectations of customers is imperative.

Many people ask, "How am I expected to do all this and still deliver the financial numbers?" or "How can I bring my staff up to speed quickly so that I can concentrate on other important business areas?" These and similar questions will be discussed throughout the book.

CHAPTER 1

PURPOSE OF PERFORMANCE MANAGEMENT

"Wisdom begins in wonder."
—SOCRATES, ANCIENT Greek Philosopher

PURPOSE IS ONE OF THE more stable elements of the PERFORMANCE framework as it looks at the reasons for having a performance management system. While looking at the purpose, it is important to ask whether the purpose can also be achieved through other means, and if so, one should carry out a cost-benefit analysis of the different alternatives. A key task here is to ensure that the purpose of the performance management system is aligned to the purpose of the organisation.

If the organisation's purpose is "to serve marginalised communities," for example, the performance management system should develop organisational capability to address the needs of the most vulnerable members of society. It should also empower employees who best serve marginalised communities, and even more so if serving those marginalised communities is also in the interest of the said employees. The purpose of the performance management system is usually denoted in terms of the human resource activities that are affected, namely rewards and recognition, career progression, training and development. Organisations should also consider the purpose of the organisation here and ensure that the performance management system, while achieving its intermediate ends, is firmly rooted in the overall purpose of the organisation. The purpose has to be effectively communicated to all stakeholders in order to ensure that people are clear on why they are carrying out certain activities.

Performance management is a philosophy by which the aspirations and objectives of individual employees are aligned to those of the organisation. The alignment process is achieved either intentionally, through planning and follow-up activities, or accidentally through personal initiative. The dichotomy of intentional versus accidental attunement to the higher-level needs of an organisation creates a variety of philosophical approaches. A laisser-faire philosophy, for example, is one in which managers allow employees to carry out their duties without any external standards or directives. As the name suggests, they let them do what they think is required for successful accomplishment of job tasks. This is in contrast with the management-led philosophy, in which managers according to their own indications guide employees in achieving set goals.

Performance Management Philosophy

The performance management philosophy that an organisation or its management adopts greatly affects performance improvement efforts, reward, recognition, development and innovation. A philosophy is a theory or attitude that acts as a guiding principle for behaviour. A performance management philosophy is, therefore, a guide in the overall approach for managing employee performance. It provides a high-level thinking or rationale of how performance is managed in a given organisation. The philosophy, like any other management thinking, must be conceived of in a framework that is linked to the purpose of an organisation.

In a laisser-faire environment, for example, the little elements that would make for a better employee experience would go unnoticed simply because those things have no one charged with handling them, in the belief that the workplace will find its own operating equilibrium. In a manager-led philosophy, employee experience is not considered because it is not believed to be a direct contributor to the bottom line, even though research has proven that employees who feel better about the workplace tend to have positive feelings associated with their work. An executive-led philosophy, insofar as it is open to influence from the external world, takes into account emerging trends and practices and is willing to experiment on their applicability within the organisation. Ideas of greatest value to an organisation are not the ones in the interior, but those that reside outside, or on the boundaries. Tapping into these ideas allows for the creation of distributed innovation systems and new business models. The value of doing this puts pressure on closed organisations.

The performance management philosophy can be planned or accidental and has a direct impact on the quality of work and productivity of an organisation. In totality, therefore, it is not possible to have two organisations that have the same performance management philosophy—or if they do, the ways they interpret it and put it into action will always differ.

Before proceeding on the types of philosophies that influence our performance management and performance improvement activities, I would like to point out that even though the philosophical approach might not be articulated as I do here, it is evident in the way managers and executives approach the subject. It is also worth noting that because the philosophical approach is an inherent reasoning behind one's actions, its results are viewed in the external world just like our beliefs influence our culture and work results.

Since performance management is a philosophy for managing the behaviour of people within a context that facilitates and supports alignment of individual goals with organisational goals in order to achieve organisational and financial performance, it is best to spell it out. This alignment has, at its very core, the balance between the needs and expectations of multiple stakeholders while matching employee performance to customer expectations and needs. It was common for organisations to operate in silos and manage their internal operations with little regard to the external environment. This way of working has become outdated due to the increased globalization, stakeholder interests, shareholder demands and competitive forces.

Before proceeding with the discussion on various performance management philosophies, it is important to pause and ask the following questions: Can an organisation effectively manage performance without a performance management philosophy? Can a manager drive employee performance without a rationale behind his actions? The answer to both is in the negative. Our thinking is related to our beliefs, and this in turn drives action. A performance management philosophy deals with the behaviour of people, and since organisations cannot do away with people management until robots have fully taken over the workplace, they have to manage individual and group behaviour. Secondly, a performance management philosophy considers the context in which the organisation operates. Performance targets are derived from an organisation's strategy, and strategy seeks to align the organisation to its internal and external environment by taking into account the real degrees of freedom that the organisation can adapt. Failure to have a performance management philosophy is equivalent to ignoring the strategic thrust of your organisation. Thirdly, the performance management philosophy facilitates the alignment of individual and organisational goals. It does this not only by determining the order of importance of goals but also by consciously managing that order. The fourth reason for having a performance management philosophy is that it makes performance management goal oriented. Performance management is not done for its own sake but for the sake of achieving predefined organisational and financial objectives. Though the actual performance management is not a philosophical endeavor, the thinking behind it is and, thus, there are a number of performance management philosophies, which I discuss.

Laisser-Faire

A *laisser-faire performance management philosophy* is one in which employees are allowed to do whatever they want, provided what they want does not disrupt the work of the organisation or that of their fellow workers. Employees are "allowed" to work without managerial intervention. In such organisations there is suboptimal production as employees can get away with anything simply because nothing was previously defined. The laisser-faire nature comes from the fact that there is no performance management system and there is no effort at aligning individual performance to organisational expectations. Employees clamour for salary and wage increments, as the organisation is welfare driven and maintains its equilibrium by trying to please the employees at all costs. One might think that such organisations do not exist, but the reality is that they do and some of them are large corporations or public entities. A belief of managers in such organisations is that employees have contracts and job descriptions which detail what is expected of them at work. They, therefore, argue that there is no need for any intervention in between the performance periods, as the employees themselves voluntarily joined the organisation without any coercion and they therefore know what is expected of them. All that is required is an annual performance review to comply with internal policies.

The laisser-faire performance management philosophy tends to use trait-based performance evaluations. The same performance evaluation form can be used throughout the organisation for all jobs. In trait-rating methods, managers evaluate employees on underlying characteristics (or traits) such as dependability, ability to work with others and leadership. Trait methods include graphic rating scales and the essay method. Graphic rating scales ask the manager to evaluate the employee on a series of scales. The rater chooses a number, a descriptive category or a point on the scale that best describes the employee. The organisation might provide the rater with a brief definition of the trait being evaluated—beyond that, the rater usually receives little guidance from the organisation about how the trait might operate in the work context or how to evaluate employee performance in terms of the trait.

Another option in the trait methods category involves asking managers to write an essay or a narrative describing the performance of each employee. Usually, raters are instructed to address the employee's strengths and weaknesses in terms of a handful of dimensions (dependability, ability to work with others and leadership are typical dimensions) and make recommendations for the employee's further development. These development opportunities include training that the employee should pursue.

One of the key drawbacks of adopting this philosophy is that employees will not know how well they are performing as individuals or even how the traits assessed contribute to organisational success. The results of any performance review are bound to meet with resistance and complaints. Another disadvantage is that the entity will not be able to break new ground, as the status quo will always prevail over the need for change. In the long run, the organisation might be unable to meet the needs of its stakeholders and customers. The organisation may also be unable to meet the employee needs of significance, growth and contribution. Employees value an environment in which they feel that they are making a worthwhile contribution. This goes with the practice of feedback and positive reinforcement, which are lacking when the organisation adopts a laisser-faire philosophy. Employees also do not feel like they are contributing because no matter how much or how little they do, the rewards and recognition remain the same. The advantage of simplicity and minor managerial involvement is completely offset by the fact that the results such a philosophy brings can be neither predicted nor foreseen. It is a working culture that is similar to working on chance and luck.

Management Led

The *management-led performance philosophy* aims to achieve organisational goals by focusing solely on the manager's intervention. These interventions are directed towards the employees. The manager is at the centre of everything that has to do with performance management. This includes the development of frameworks and tools, administering the tools and making performance-based decisions. The manager in this case could be an individual or a group of managers who come together to exercise judgment in matters relating to performance management. In extreme cases this manager is the HR manager, who is charged with the responsibility of driving all aspects of performance management with little or no support from the executives. I refer to this as an "extreme case" because the HR manager is not suited to developing goals and performance tools for individual departments without input from functional specialists. There are certain tasks that need to be left to individual line managers. Typically, what happens is that HR managers develop performance appraisal forms which they distribute to other managers and request to have completed. This exercise of completing performance appraisal forms can be done by the manager on his own or with input from his staff within a given timeline. The managers who receive this request act upon it as requested and distribute the appraisal forms to their staff who in turn complete and submit them to their managers for final assessment and comments. This approach is used by very many organisations, and among other challenges it faces a lot of resistance and differences in interpretations from employees. If the manager is lenient he will have a seemingly happy workforce whose major complaint is the lack of challenge. If the manager is strict there will be many complaints from employees who feel that they have not been treated justly in the appraisal and development process.

It is important to note here that what gets assessed is based on the manager's feeling or on some agreement that was made at the beginning of the year with not much thought or structured analysis taking place. The managers or management group that is responsible for the implementation of performance management practices draw their strength from the appointing authority or from widespread practice. There is a belief that since this is how it is done in many organisations, it is the right way of doing things. On one hand the HR department would like to have evidence that the performance of employees is being periodically reviewed, hence the appraisal forms, and on the other hand the appointing authority would like some assurance that things are being done as they should be done.

The management-led philosophy is very much focused on ranking employees and comparing them with each other. You will therefore find that organisations that adopt this philosophy tend to favour the performance evaluation methods of ranking systems and forced distributions. A ranking system involves directly ranking employees within a department or unit. A manager or supervisor will identify the best employee followed by the second best and so forth for all the employees. A forced distribution requires managers to group the employees they supervise.

Comparative performance evaluation methods are becoming more popular as organisations are asked to make difficult downsizing and promotion decisions.

Although comparative systems can be useful for administrative purposes, they fall short in terms of providing developmental feedback to employees. Learning that your supervisor ranked you twentieth out of fifty employees (in a ranking system) or receiving a B grade (in a forced distribution) provides little information about how to improve performance. Just as with graphic rating scales, the burden of supplementing comparative methods with developmental feedback falls to the supervisor or manager.

While the management-led performance philosophy makes improvements on the laisser-faire philosophy in terms of driving performance as opposed to waiting for things to happen on their own, it has one major drawback: misalignment with the needs and interests of the executives, customers and other key stakeholders. It does not make reference to the organisation's strategy and lacks executive power to implement decisions related to development, rewards and recognition. While managers play the role of being the link between executives and staff, this link is somewhat watered down when the executive is not fully involved in setting the tone of performance management practices. The alignment is lost over time because what remains is the prevailing need for employees to work according to the wishes of management.

Another drawback of this philosophy is that management is not usually in direct contact with the company's external stakeholders, such as regulators or even shareholders. External stakeholders are usually in the purview of the executive. This means that it would take longer to respond to the needs of such external constituents because of lack of direct and regular contact. For this philosophy to deliver excellent results, a lot depends on the quality of the managers who oversee the performance management process and their ability to imagine the future of the organisation and to engage in strategic thinking. Many managers have at some point in their working lives espoused the laisser-faire philosophy knowingly or unknowingly. A manager may ignore performance discussions with his staff for an extended period of time, either because he feels the employee is not worth the effort or that the employee is doing well on his own and does not require external intervention. Other times managers feel pressed for time and selectively engage with their high-performing staff and ignore the lower performers, leaving them to their own discretion. In the latter case employees who are left out of their managers' attention feel the organisation is selective and practices favouritism. All employees have a sense of pride and want to feel that they have a contribution to make in the organisation. In the case of low performers managers need to implement employee development plans and support the employees in addressing their performance gaps through a variety of interventions.

Executive Led

The *executive-led performance philosophy* argues that for performance management to be effective there must be a linkage between the purpose for which the organisation exists and its strategic goals and objectives. As the name suggests, this philosophy depends on an active involvement by the executives in all aspects of performance management from strategy-goal congruence to feedback, measurement, monitoring, reviewing and updating. The rationale behind this philosophy is that the organisation exists to serve a predetermined purpose or need and that the executives are the custodians of that interest. By being the custodians of that interest, they ensure that management systems are in place to guarantee that the work carried out in the organisation seeks to serve its formational purpose. The executive is not a silent onlooker in the game of performance management but an active player, arbiter and coach. An organisation might use different frameworks for performance management, but these systems need to be developed with input from the executives. The executives are involved in selecting the framework, developing the tools, communicating the selected system to staff and ensuring compliance and active involvement of all staff. They're involved in the development of rewards and recognition systems as well as in arbitrating on performance disputes and disagreements. They also decide on matters within the system that can be customised to the needs of different departments and those that can be personalised according to the needs of employees. If certain aspects of the system are to be automated, the executives will also be involved in selecting and/or approving the technology platform and dashboard software that will be used. The executive is also a consumer of performance information through dashboards and other types of periodic reports.

In terms of performance appraisal methods, those who hold the executive-led performance philosophy tend to favour result-oriented methods, such as management by objectives and the balanced scorecard. This is because these methods are tailored to individual employees' needs and abilities. They are therefore excellent for providing developmental feedback, though they are not very useful for administrative decisions because employees are not evaluated on a similar scale. That administrative drawback is addressed through the use of forums that evaluate the contributions of individuals to their departments, evaluated on different scales. This evaluation is also carried out with respect to the department's contribution to the achievement of organisational goals and objectives.

The key advantage of the executive-led performance philosophy is the fact that it fosters alignment between the organisation and its external stakeholders. Shareholders, for example, have a direct way of expressing their interests or demands through the executives who are hired to work in the interests of the shareholders. In a similar manner, the executive also ensures that the organisation is in touch with its customers and regulators, and responds promptly to the needs of these stakeholders.

A bank, for example, that adopts this philosophy might be required by the Central or Reserve Bank to increase its capital. This increase in capital requirements might be addressed through reducing their risk-weighted assets or by increasing their levels of regulatory capital. If a bank opts not to raise its levels of equity, the result of this might be reduced lending to corporate and retail customers, resulting in lower asset, investment and sales growth. Thus, the regulatory requirement on capital adequacy has resulted in an action that has affected the performance of the retail and corporate departments that proactively sell bank loans in order to keep the bank solvent.

The table below highlights the key differences between the three performance management philosophies.

FEATURE	LAISSER-FAIRE	MANAGEMENT-LED	EXECUTIVE-LED
Performance planning	No planning takes place	Managers plan for appraisals	Planning is linked to the strategy
Periodicity of performance-improvement activities	Only during annual appraisals	During appraisals	All year round using a variety of methods and tools
Involvement	Staff	Managers and staff	Executives, managers and staff
Focus on customers	No	Sometimes	Intrinsically
Focus on stakeholders	No	No	Yes
Measures and recognises	Traits	Efforts	Results
Linked to strategy	No	Sometimes	Always
Tools used to manage performance	Simple appraisal form	Appraisal forms and annual calendar	A number of tools including forms, dashboards, coaching, reviews and alignment sessions
Appraisal method	Trait based	Ranking and comparisons	Results based
Documentation of performance evidence	Manual records	Both manual and computerised	Largely automated

FEATURE	LAISSER-FAIRE	MANAGEMENT-LED	EXECUTIVE-LED
Performance improvement methods used	Limited use of training	Training and selective use of job aids	Extensive training, performance customisation and personalisation, coaching, job aids, standards, workplace rules and procedures
Types of rewards offered	Salaries and benefits	Salaries and benefits	Salaries, benefits, long- and short-term incentive schemes, spot awards and many others

Case Study 1: Genie Catalyst's Performance Approach

Genie Catalyst is a service company that has existed for a long time. It develops forms that employees discuss with their managers as a basis of performance review. Their performance review process consisted of a discussion between the manager and subordinates on expectations for the year, and a review at the middle of the year; but due to work demands the mid-year review was rarely enforced, and compliance levels were very low. At the end of the year the manager and his staff met and discussed the performance around the agreed objectives and goals. This process was fraught with a lot of challenges. In many cases there was no reference to the agreed goals during the year; neither was there an attempt from either the employees or managers to find out what progress had been made against the agreed goals. The result was discontent from employees who felt that their efforts were not appreciated and managers who tried to force down their assessments on employees.

The directors of Genie Catalyst discovered that the process had inherent challenges, and without consulting either the employees or managers decided to change certain elements of the performance management system. The first thing they did was christen the performance management system, and then they developed a number of forms with predefined content based on the principles and design of the balanced scorecards. The forms were prescribed for use to all managers, and there was little leeway in changing the content or the weighing of the aspects that had been predefined. The practice of midyear appraisals continued, but compliance rates remained low. At the end of the year a review forum in which the executives participated took place. The aim of the session was for managers to present the appraisals of their staff to the rest of the managers and executives with a view to gain concurrence on ratings. The forum was meant to be a confidential forum; however, some managers disclosed to respective staff comments that had been made about them and how these had contributed to their ratings. When staff received their feedback from the session a good number of them disagreed with the results, and many left the company. This review-exit phenomenon has now been going on for a number of years.

Can you identify what performance management philosophy this company was using? Why were there so many challenges?

Performance management philosophy has moved from management control and direction, through coercion, to one based on shared values such as participation and empowerment. This is one of the reasons that even the organisations that adopt a management-led philosophy have to modify it to take into account the participatory needs of employees. Performance management is less bureaucratic. More and more organisations are reviewing the need for formal ranking mechanisms which limit employee creativity by boxing them in a category. In Case Study 1 about Genie Catalyst, there was a lot of bureaucracy in the performance management process, and employees felt that they were being coerced into acting. Managers also felt coerced but did not speak out as they feared the ramifications.

Each employee's unique knowledge, skills, experience and personal style are essential to achieving the objectives of the organisation. A performance management philosophy should not only be based on the senior executives but should also consider the unique contributions that employees, through their skills, experience and insights, are able to bring to bear on the process. This is the reason why, in executive-led philosophy, executives are responsible for communicating the performance management system to employees and for ensuring that the employee voice has been heard throughout the process. They also provide room for customisation and personalisation in order to allow the uniqueness of each department and individual to shine through. It is a given that each employee, being different from one another, will have a lot to offer in aiding the organisation to achieve its objectives. Each employee also brings in an element of creativity in the achievement of the organisational objectives, since for many activities there is more than one way in which the results can be achieved in an ethical and coordinated manner. This opportunity to include employee contribution not only leads to their individual growth but also promotes employee engagement and staff retention.

Empowerment and participation of employees in the workplace is essential for the employee's well-being and for motivating the employees to commit to the objectives of the organisation. The performance management practices that empower an employee to give his best at work are the same ones that result in reduced turnover and reduced complaints because employees will feel that their contribution matters.

Embedding Philosophy in Policy

The performance management philosophy that an organisation adopts should be embedded in its policy. A performance management policy is a system of principles to guide decision-making and derive rational outcomes in the area of performance management. It provides a set of guiding principles to help with decision-making in the area of performance management and explains the responsibilities associated with its implementation. Policies are usually implemented with procedures. The policy is generally approved by the executive in most organisations or the board. The Society for Human Resources Management (SHRM) provides the purpose of a performance management policy: it says that the performance appraisal provides a means for discussing, planning and reviewing the performance of each employee. In so doing, the society states, regular appraisals are useful in helping employees clearly define and understand their responsibilities, providing criteria by which employees' performance will be evaluated, suggesting ways in which employees can improve performance, identifying employees with potential for advancement within the organisation, helping managers distribute and achieve departmental goals and providing a fair basis for awarding compensation based on merit.

Organisations need to have a performance management policy, which outlines the responsibility for performance management. It should also provide guidance on how each of the key activities of the performance calendar should be managed and who will be responsible for their execution. Some of the procedures that should be mentioned or defined in the policy include: strategy-cascading procedures; procedure for collecting, collating, analyzing, giving and receiving feedback; procedure for moderation of performance ratings; procedure for performance rewards and procedure for changing or adapting goals in between the performance management cycles.

Performance management, just like any other management discipline, is a process. It cannot be considered an instant or form-filling exercise. The planning process starts with goal setting between an employee and a supervisor. Managers have challenges in the goal-setting process because they are not sure to what extent the employee expectations or aspirations should supersede organisational goals. A manager knows that he has to achieve certain goals, and to do so requires the collaboration and execution of tasks by his subordinates. Therefore, it is important for both parties to strike a balance between the two extremes. Employee interests should not supersede those of the organisation, neither should they be totally ignored. Customisation then becomes an important ingredient in the performance management process for just as it is exercised and planned for in relation to customers it must also be taken care of in the case of employees. Managers also need to organise their staff and teams in a way that allows them to perform at a superior level. They need to ensure that their teams are optimally staffed for best results and that the manager regularly oversees and directs work. Managers are also responsible for preparing periodic performance reports, which are submitted to the executives. The reports should describe not only what results have been obtained but how they have been obtained. Technology tools and dashboards exist to support managers in this task.

Ultimately it might seem that each of the three performance management philosophies are really a subset of the executive-led philosophy because, in each of them, someone has to be behind the approach and someone has to approve the approach to performance improvement. It is therefore important for executives to be aware that whatever they say or don't say has a profound impact on the initiatives that managers carry out in improving business performance. Whatever the executive pays attention to and what he does not pay attention to determines what managers and staff will pay attention to. If the executive does not pay attention to developing and maturing the organisation's performance management system, the role will be left to someone either accidentally or intentionally, and the results of such efforts will always tend to be suboptimal due to the lack of executive sponsorship, direction and buy-in.

There is no clear-cut distinction of the type of leaders that the performance management philosophy brings up because leadership by its very nature is affected by many variables. What is clear though is that the degree of openness and tolerance for ambiguity and fluidity is much higher in the executive-led philosophy. This is so because this philosophy is not centred only on the internal determinants of performance and success but also on the external ones that underpin strategic posturing. Strategy orientation is very important for the success of organisations, and so are the performance management practices and philosophy that are linked to such orientations. One might ask whether it is possible to take the best aspects of each of the three performance management philosophies and fuse them into one. This is akin to asking if it is possible to bring together scientific management in its approach to human work to that of the human relations school. There certainly are some elements from each philosophy that can work together, but many times establishing such a blend might reduce focus on results and cause confusion.

Some organisations have developed appraisal instruments, for example, which contain a section on results to be achieved, a section on behaviours or traits to be demonstrated and a moderation system which ranks employees relative to each other. In addition, there might be a section requiring commentaries or rating of employee behaviour relative to organisational values. If this fusion is not managed and communicated well to all parties, it could result in employee confusion, especially when the traits suggest that the employee's performance meets expectations while the results do not. A case in point could be an organisation assessing employee timekeeping, deportment and communication without relating these traits to business results such as increase in customer satisfaction, reduction in customer complaints or resolving customer complaints in a timely manner. In ranking such an employee against others there must be an objective way to use results, behaviours or both. Such an approach would involve determining behaviours that lead to desired results and using the attained results as a basis of ranking, assuming that the behaviours have been of the right type and undesirable behaviours or shortcuts eliminated.

Case Study 2: Prosperity Bank's Usage of Performance Management Philosophy during Transformation

Prosperity Bank is a large commercial bank that was undergoing transformation as a result of declining market share and employee dissatisfaction. It has always ranked first or second nationally in terms of assets, but ongoing staff disillusionment made the bank rethink its performance management practices. It, therefore, felt that it was important to integrate the views of the executive in performance management discussions so as to give more credibility to the process in the eyes of staff. The bank had been stable for many years; however, now it faced a number of challenges including high employee attrition and levels of dissatisfaction. There were also business opportunities which were prevalent in the market, but managers did not seize them and they tended to be targeted by competitors or dissipate with time.

The bank realised that it, therefore, needed to strengthen its performance management system to go beyond simply entrusting the performance of the bank to managers and staff. It realised the importance of providing direction and impetus to the performance management process and inculcating an executive-led philosophy. The process started by the bank hiring a consultant and working with the consultant to develop training content and courses for its senior managers in the area of performance management. The trainings sought to equip the managers with knowledge on the principles and practices of an executive-led performance management system and process. They then provided the output of these trainings to the executives in the form of an outcomes briefing which also highlighted the areas in which they expected the business to see improvements. After a period of six months, the executive team became more involved in performance discussions, articulated the bank's strategy better and approved an investment in automation of the performance management system. The executives are since fully involved and aligned and own the performance management and improvement agenda. After one year the bank's top-line revenue grew by more than 20 percent from improved performance management practices. The new CEO of the bank is fully involved in promoting a performance culture by leading performance discussions and showcasing individuals and teams who demonstrate the desired and aligned behaviours.

Performance Management Philosophy and Strategy

The selected performance management philosophy has a direct impact on the pursuit of an organisation's strategy. Strategy implementation is a journey that starts with an examination of where we are and where we want to go. It then asks the question, "What do we need to do in order to get where we want to go?"

The bridge between where we are and where we want to go is the subject of strategy implementation, in which different approaches have been proposed and written about. Most organisations take a strategy and break it down to goals and objectives which are then assigned to their respective departments. An organisation, for example, which has a strategy of "being the best employer" may have as its goal "to attract and retain the best talent in the market." This goal would then be assigned to the human resources department, who would act as the custodian of the goal and its implementation. As part of implementation the department would review the systems it has for recruiting and managing talent with a view of ensuring that internal systems do not inhibit it from achieving the stated goal.

Other organisations will examine the behaviours that employees and managers need to exhibit in order to achieve the stated goals. In the previous example of "being the best employer," the organisation would identify the behaviours employees need to exhibit to show that it is making progress towards achieving the stated goal. These behaviours could range from "retaining 5 percent of the top talent"—which is a measurable target that implies managers are aware of who comprises "top talent" and that they are doing things to keep that top talent through engagement—to "providing monthly proactive feedback to top talent." Competitive advantage can be derived from any number of sources in today's organisations. Superior strategies, innovative products and exemplary customer service are just some of the many ways in which organisations seek to differentiate themselves from others. But for some organisations, the way they behave is what makes the difference and provides the source of their strength. Values are the timeless principles that guide an organisation. They represent the deeply held beliefs within an organisation and are demonstrated through the day-to-day behaviours of all employees. An organisation's values make an open proclamation about how it expects everyone to behave.

The performance management philosophy, since it is an approach for managing myriad performance management activities, has a direct relationship with the strategy process and with the outcomes of the strategy process as highlighted in the table below:

Table 4 : Link between Strategy and Performance Management Philosophy

ASPECT OF STRATEGY	LAISSER-FAIRE	MANAGEMENT-LED	EXECUTIVE-LED
Strategy development	Everyone develops their own strategy	Managers develop the strategy	Executives develop the strategy in consultation with stakeholders
Environmental scanning	Not carried out	Not carried out	Is part and parcel of the strategy and renewal process
Internal capability analysis	Not carried out	Not carried out	Is part and parcel of the strategy process
Assignment of objectives	Everyone chooses what they want to do	Management assigns objectives	Executives determine and assign objectives to functional groups
Objective measurement	Rarely done	Management tracks and measures some objectives	Sophisticated dashboards and tools are used to measure objective performance
Review and change in objectives	Rarely done	Done every three to five years	Done as and when the stakeholder needs and the environmental realities warrant
Performance appraisal	Uses what is seen or claimed by the employee	Uses a two-way, consensus-building process	Includes multiple sources including customers, regulators and other stakeholders
Link between performance and training	First come, first served	Choices are based on manager favourites and available budget	Choices are based on current and potential roles and impact on strategic objectives

ASPECT OF STRATEGY	LAISSER-FAIRE	MANAGEMENT-LED	EXECUTIVE-LED
Link between performance and reward	No link; all employees are treated equally	Managers make proposals for consideration	Policies determine how rewards get allocated and tools are used to harmonise and implement changes
Coverage of strategic elements	Partially, as there is limited awareness of all elements of the strategy	Partially, as managers select what they wish to implement	Total; tools and techniques are used to ensure complete coverage of all strategic elements

The vibrancy of an organisation is not achieved solely by attaining sales or financial targets. These achievements are important, but focusing solely on them does not make a vibrant organisation but a "trophy-chasing entity" where employees come and go leaving little evidence of impact. In the knowledge economy, it is about attracting, retaining and growing talent. Knowledge workers not only want to be paid well and receive competitive benefits, but they increasingly demand a vibrant and vital workplace. Vibrant organisations exist to create a legacy that outlives incumbents. Such vibrancy is created by the long-term nature of the strategy process and promoting long-term thinking over short-term financial gain and benefits. This long-term thinking requires conscious leadership and holding ongoing conversations about the work of employees and its importance to the organisation and the wider community. It also requires the provision of new learning and stretch assignments, engaging employees in challenges facing their organisations and implementing flexible approaches to managing work and performance.

To be effective, the performance management process must be firmly linked to and rooted in the organisation's strategy. Strategy involves the formulation of the organisation's mission, goals, objectives and action plans for achievement. Every employee must share in this. The key is to clearly articulate each employee's goals, objectives and competency requirements in a way that will facilitate the successful achievement of the organisation's strategy. Adopting a laisser-faire or management-led performance management philosophy might jeopardise strategy success both in the short and in the long term.

CHAPTER 2

THE EMPLOYEE IN THE PERFORMANCE MANAGEMENT EQUATION

*"It is not from the benevolence of the butcher, the brewer, or the baker, that
we expect our dinner, but from their regard to their own interest."*
—ADAM SMITH, The Wealth of Nations

STELLA WAS AN EXECUTIVE WHO enjoyed reading and self-development. She had worked in many organisations, deputizing as different heads of the institutions. She had not yet worked as a chief executive, but an opportunity to become a chief executive came, and she found herself in an organisation which seemed to be in need of a number of improvements—including its strategic orientation, state of the working environment, branding and employee capability. Faced with these challenges, Stella developed a plan to improve the organisational performance using the available resources. To do this she determined which improvement actions could be carried out using internal resources and capability and set off carrying out these activities. She aligned the employees to the plan by showing them how the required improvements were in their hands. This ability to share the organisational development plan with her staff led to resounding success and public acclaim. She was able to align the employees to her vision and to the mandate that had been entrusted to her.

Employees are an important pillar in the performance management framework. The role of employees in carrying out performance management activities beyond merely being recipients is examined in this chapter. Employees should be provided with the right sort of orientation based on their level, roles and experience with performance management systems.

The performance management philosophy is the starting point in the establishment of a performance management system. This is followed by ensuring that the performance management system and its parameters are designed to support the achievement of the strategic objectives of the organisation. Once this has been done, the next step is to determine how the organisation intends to utilise the capability of the employees to achieve its objectives. In a laisser-faire performance management setup, I demonstrated how the employee is left on his own to figure things out. This section is devoted to showing the reader how employee capability can be better harnessed not only to achieve the goals and objectives of the organisation but also to ensure that the employees for their part are fulfilled and engaged with the mission of the organisation by achieving their own objectives.

First of all, it's important to remember that performance management is about developing employees, and that development is first and foremost in the interest of the employee, the subject of development. Regardless of the philosophy employed you must give certain attention to the things the employee does and how they are done.

Starting with Career Discussions

The first step of aligning employees to the organisation's strategy is to find out what employees intend to achieve through the employment opportunity. Employees join organisations first because they would like a source of livelihood, but after that they continually ask if the organisation is the right one for them in terms of their career direction, growth and opportunities. An entity can bring forward this discussion with employees by discussing employee career aspirations and how employee expectations are fully or partially met through the achievement of the strategic objectives of the organisation.

At Genie Catalyst, there was a move to enhance diverse workforce segments including ensuring that different professions had good representations of male and female employees. In the service department there was a relatively large number of females compared to males. One of these males, David, was a recent graduate and had a keen interest in growing his career. He was interested in academics but had been in the organisation for only a year; hence, his true worth had not been fully realised or observed. In career discussions, his manager found that he was interested in becoming a lecturer and in pursuing further studies which would allow him to be employed in an institution of higher learning. The manager had some tasks that involved instructional design and training, and she assigned them to him as this tied in well with his career ambition and even acted as a catalyst in some way. David appreciated the work and showed high levels of commitment for the next two years before proceeding to further studies, after which he joined an institution of higher learning as a tutorial assistant. The manager was able to connect his interests to the organisation's just in time and to further the employee's personal development, even if it ended up being outside the organisation.

One of the most essential tasks in the entire strategy process is to link the strategic pursuit to the achievement of results in the real world and to employee activities. This requires simple and clear measures of success. It also requires an equitable framework and involvement of all stakeholders in the process.

The target results should be developed to match the descriptions of your business or of your organisation. Financial results, strategic balance sheets, operating results, organisational changes, total enterprise value and share price targets can all be set as the objectives of your strategy program. The results of individual initiatives and the overall performance of the business should be spelled out to ensure that the impact is measured and that the strategy is indeed aimed at driving the performance of the business on a tangible basis to greater performance and success.

In addition to increasing performance in competitive, financial, and operational areas, strategy reviews the need to broaden the definition of success for a modern business.

By including a different set of measures, business leaders can build a stronger and more enduring enterprise. External measures that reflect a broader engagement in community and ecology can be captured in new standards of triple-bottom-line accounting. Internal measures of employee satisfaction, retention of desirable employees, intellectual capital development, brand value and alliance capability are also potentially important measures. Including a different set of measures should not be done for the sake of external benchmarking only but should be based on the actual needs and requirements of the organisation.

These results being tracked should be specific and measurable wherever possible and should be backed by initiatives. Initiatives should identify in advance the required support, interlinked initiatives and organisational dependencies. If the initiatives do not identify these things in advance they will fail to be implemented or experience delays and cost overruns. Authority and required authorizations need to be clearly spelled out so individuals and groups know where their authority starts and ends.

In the spirit of focusing on priorities and investing differentially in a select set of levers on performance and value, it is useful to confirm that there is at least one target result for each lever and priority identified in the strategy.

In the last chapter I discussed how strategy and purpose are the key drivers of performance. In this chapter I'm going to break down how to use strategy and purpose to drive performance. I will show you the eleven elements to take into consideration as you develop goals with your employees that align with the strategy, and how to bring all that together with a carefully planned SMART program that clearly conveys expectations to employees.

Managers should seek to understand the organisation's strategy and share that understanding with their staff. They should also ensure that they are fully aware of the role that their departments or units are responsible for in the context of achieving the strategic objectives. Managers should then set goals with the employees who work in their departments. They should not set goals for the employees. Involving employees in the goal-setting process is critical. The purpose of setting goals is to give employees agreed targets on which to focus. If the employee has not participated in the establishment of these goals, they are less likely to buy in to the goals and less likely to find them motivating. There are a variety of formats that a manager can use to cocreate goals with his employees, and these are discussed in this section.

Setting Mutually Agreeable Goals

Setting mutually agreeable goals with employees should be a positive process. It allows both the manager and employee to share hopes and ideas for the future. Setting goals will lead to higher levels of performance and result in more motivated employees.

A manager who is ready to develop goals with his employees should start by setting time aside to talk with the employee in private without interruptions or distractions. This demonstrates that you as the manager are vested in the process and that you take it seriously. Every employee knows that when a manager asks to see him in private there is an important issue to be discussed.

Once you have scheduled time with your staff member, prepare a draft of goals for him in advance and ask him to create a similar draft based on the strategic direction the organisation or department is pursuing, his interests and job description and other tasks that he undertakes in the organisation. In preparing your draft goals to discuss with your staff member, it is advisable for you to review the following sources of performance goals. The list of sources is quite long and detailed, but it is not my opinion that managers should use all the elements when formulating goals for their employees; rather, armed with this information, the manager should look at the relative importance of each of these sources given the prevailing circumstances in the organisation and given the capability of the employee. It will therefore happen in some cases that an employee has no projects underway, and this type of goal will be replaced with a problem-solving one, for example. There needs to be some internal agreement about how many and which types of goals managers should set for their employees, taking into account each employee's seniority, role, capabilities and skills.

Here is a list of places to start from when working on employee goals:

- Company's strategy, mission and objectives by describing the overall goals and objectives of the organisation.

- Routine job functions or work objectives by referring to the employee's position or job description. For example, a maintenance engineer should ensure that all machinery is kept in good working condition.

- Targets by developing quantifiable goals that should be met such as ensuring 100 percent machinery availability each week.

- Problem-solving issues by identifying any known problems that need to be solved. For example, reducing chemical wastage in the factory.

- Tasks or projects by determining the specified results or product (e.g., a new maintenance guide to be developed in two weeks).

- Behavioural expectations by outlining desirable and undesirable behaviours (e.g., excellent customer service to be provided at the front desk at all times).

- Values by providing descriptors that outline the values of the organisation.

- New innovative ideas by detailing what developments should be delivered.

- Individual employee development needs or performance improvement areas, like skills, knowledge, experience (e.g., improvement needed in database management).

- Developmental/learning by providing specific areas to meet individual improvement needs.

- Department or unit's objectives by providing information on the unit's mandate and objectives that are linked to the organisation's goals.

Let us discuss each of these sources of goals and how and when they should be used in the goal-setting process. As you go through the descriptions below, take note that you do not need to use each source for each employee during each performance period. The relative importance of the source of goals should be assessed against the company's policy on the number of goals an employee will have during a given period, the employee's own capacity to manage multiple goals and the relative importance of the given area in improving individual performance during the period.

The Company Strategy

The first source and perhaps the most important is the company's strategy, mission and objectives. The company's strategy stipulates the ends that the organisation seeks to achieve. The strategy determines the allocation of resources and directs the actions of employees and managers in the pursuit of common goals. It defines the expected results to be achieved in the long term and defines measures that enable the organisation to manage its performance to achieve those results.

A *mission statement* defines the company's business, its objectives and its approach to reach those objectives. A *vision statement* describes the desired future position of the company. Elements of mission and vision statements are often combined to provide a statement of the company's purposes, goals and values. These elements are usually formulated in such a way that they lead to the formulation of strategic objectives and plans together with the required resources to achieve those plans. The strategy may be documented or not, but it has to be shared by the organisation's leaders. A review of the strategy will help managers set goals for employees that make the employees work in a manner that is supportive of achieving the vision and mission of the organisation. It is not enough to set a goal or goals that support the organisation's mission; the manager should ensure that there is a way of tracking the performance against those goals and documenting the employee accomplishments during the performance review sessions. One way of doing this is to have a section in the appraisal form that relates to the accomplishments that employees made in supporting the organisation to achieve its mission. It could be a question asking managers to list activities the employee carried out that supported the company mission in the last year or the last couple of months.

The Job Description

The job description is a list of duties that the jobholder is expected to carry out on a day-to-day basis. The job description is not a static document but changes as the job requirements change due to organisational changes or even changes in the business processes, interactions and other external factors that affect the job content. There are many formats for writing job descriptions, but these are outside the scope of this book. Our interest here is to guide managers on how to use job descriptions in the goal-setting process. There are also a number of standards on what should or should not be included in the job description. Some organisations include only the major tasks that the jobholder should carry out, while others include a detailed listing of the job content. Whichever format your organisation uses, you need to refer to the approved job description when setting performance goals. Within the content of the job description, identify those duties that have the greatest contribution towards achievement of the department or unit mandate and formulate goals against those duties. You may find duties such as "Participate in the annual stakeholder's convention" to be important but to occur infrequently; this target should be combined with other similar duties in order not to have an overly aggressive or exaggerated statement of goals. It is the role of the manager to exercise discretion based on the prevailing circumstances to select those duties that have an overarching consistency and are not overly operational. The idea is that in carrying out those goals the operational duties will also be taken into account.

Thus, there is no direct correlation between the number of duties described in the job description and the number of goals that will be assigned to an employee during a given performance period.

Targets

The third source of performance goals is the targets. Targets come from a number of sources including company policy, customer expectations, regulatory requirements, office setup and managerial initiatives. Targets are also related to the company strategy, which we discussed earlier in this section.

A *target* is a predefined level of performance. A target of 98 percent system availability, for example, implies that the respective individual or department should ensure that the system is always online and available to the end users 98 percent of the time. The target is derived from the expectations that customers, employees and other stakeholders have in terms of being able to execute tasks, carry out operations or consult the system. A target that is externally initiated leaves very little room for negotiation and becomes an act of strategic compliance.

There are other targets that can be negotiated, such as the sales volumes or financial targets. The negotiation of such targets should not, however, compromise the ability of an organisation or its departments from achieving their mandate. In setting targets with employees, managers should start by finding out about any targets that the department ought to achieve and then determining how to achieve the targets with the employees at their disposal. The next thing would be to identify which of the employees has the required skills to be able to meet the set targets or which employees need to be developed in order to be able to meet the target. Armed with this information the manager can plan the goal-setting meeting with the respective employee. If the target is critical the manager should also ensure that a fall-back plan or person is available at all times. The targets that are identified can be matched with requirements from the job description in order to ensure adherence to the *raison d'être* of the particular job.

Problem-Solving Issues

The fourth source of goals is problem-solving issues. Problems abound in today's workplace, ranging from implementing a new software system, migrating from one platform to another, moving offices, changing office layout, launching a new product or service as well as making operational improvements in the workplace. A manager will therefore start by identifying the problems that need to be solved during a given performance period and then examine his staff to see which ones would be available and skilled enough to meet the demands of the problem to be solved. In relation to the job purpose, the manager can develop a problem-solving goal that is related to one or more of the job requirements which the employee has not fully demonstrated competence in or a situation-based exigency for which an employee's problem-solving skills will be assessed.

Tasks or Projects

The fifth source of goals comes from tasks or projects. Similar to the discussion above, projects come in all manner of forms, from small departmental projects to larger and complex organisation-wide projects. Irrespective of the size and complexity of the project, managers need to understand the nature of any projects their staff might be involved in as well as their contributions. It sometimes happens that the staff of department A are nominated to work in a project which is housed in department B. Both managers of the two departments should be clear about the performance expectations of the employee from department A and how this performance will be monitored, tracked and evaluated. They also need to decide who among the two managers will evaluate the employee on the project performance and the standards that will be used to evaluate them. Simply attending project meetings is not an adequate performance goal. This particular area is one which allows employee input to be considered more as there are a variety of tasks or projects within and outside the individual's department that can be carried out. These range from projects to replace a filing system, to launch a product or service, or to those related to automation of a system or capability.

Behavioural Expectations

A sixth source of goals is the behavioural expectations that a company or an entity has of its staff. Employee behaviour can either help or hurt an organisation. The term *employee behaviour* refers to the way in which employees respond to specific circumstances or situations in the workplace. While many elements determine an individual's behaviour in the workplace, employees are shaped by their culture and by the organisation's culture. Companies rely on employees to produce and deliver high-quality products and services. Employee behaviour is impacted by a variety of forces, both internal and external, as they attempt to perform their job duties. Managers and employers who are aware of these forces, and who are prepared to leverage or counteract them, can have a positive impact on the employee's behaviour. There are a number of forces that influence employee behaviour:

- *Positive environment:* A critical, internal force that influences employee behaviour is the actions of colleagues. Companies that can effectively build an internal culture that is based on mutual respect, teamwork, and support will attract and retain employees with good behaviour.

- *Technology:* Technology is a significant factor that can have both positive and disruptive influences on employee behaviour. While technology can often help streamline processes and make work easier for employees, learning how to use new technology while remaining productive can be stressful. Factor in the rapid advent of technology in general, and employers seem to be faced with an almost ongoing need for new training, process improvement, and documentation.

- *Customer demands:* Customer demands can be an external force that exert pressure on organisations to continually stay ahead of the competitive curve. Employees must adapt to the changing needs of customers, the growing shrewdness of customers and the heightened expectations that customers put on employee behaviour.

One of the largest expenses to any organisation is the cost of labour. Good managers work hard to set expectations for each employee. This is done through in-service meetings, monthly staff meetings, annual reviews and the overall culture of an organisation. It is important to use the right forum for goal setting and preferably use the same forum when you review performance against the set goals.

Managers should set the right behavioural expectations of their employees, including team norms such as actively participating in weekly meetings, arriving on time at client events and not using insulting or demeaning language towards colleagues. Behavioural norms usually pose a challenge to managers because many of them find that working with behaviours seems intangible. Faced with this challenge, a manager developed a team purpose and from it determined that one of the team behaviours was "responsiveness." He decided to discuss this in a team meeting to gain concurrence from the team on what being responsive meant. Does it mean having a set time to respond to an email or other forms of communication? The number of months, weeks, days, hours, minutes or seconds that should elapse between a request and a solution? Does it imply going out of one's way to handle a critical business issue over a routine issue?

The team agreed that these questions implied responsiveness and that as an accounting team they had to abide by their agreed standards. They then formulated these questions as statements and hung them prominently on the wall of their office as a constant reminder of the need for team members to be responsive to staff asking for details of their pay breakdown, managers requesting accounts of a new product's performance, or suppliers following up on the status of an unpaid invoice. Managers want to achieve synergy and believe that the efforts of the team should be coordinated and geared towards achieving the units' objectives. They need to drive the behaviour that leads to integration and which improves execution.

Organisational Values

The seventh source of goals is the values of the organisation. The core values are based on the principles or beliefs that the organisation views as being of central importance. These core values are set by the founders of the entity and create the identity of the entity. The key thing that managers need to remember in relation to core values is that they must be consistently applied or they run the risk of being epithets or slogans that employees recite but never put into practice.

In order to transform these beliefs and, hence, the underlying values into tangibles, managers need to create experiences that promote the organisation's core values. Managers should therefore be conscious about how they would like the values to be demonstrated through the work that employees carry out. Another way of addressing behavioural expectations is to examine the tasks employees carry out and then define the behaviours that lead to superior performance. Large restaurant chains use this approach in defining how many tables a given waiter should serve and the attributes of service that the waiter needs to show. The values of the organisation can also be tied into or linked to the other focus areas previously described. If the value of an organisation, for example, is dependability, an employee goal can be crafted by linking his role in a project to not only the project outcomes but also to demonstrating the value of dependability.

Innovative Ideas

The eighth source of goals is new innovative ideas. Law firms have been adjusting their mode of working, and many large law firms have begun creating customer service functions similar to those found in banks. The added responsibility of the customer service function in law firms is to create thought pieces and industry research that influences the work of legal teams and attracts clients. Innovation is not static, and neither are the goals developed for employees in this area. What was innovative at one point in time might be the norm in another and could yet be a matter of routine compliance. Innovative ideas are everywhere, and it is not surprising that in assigning a goal a manager may require the employee to introduce at least one innovative element in the output. There is a case of a manager who reviewed periodic reports on a company process; the reports had the same structure each time with changes only in the data and information presented. The manager assigned a goal to the employee in charge to not only produce timely and quality reports but to suggest and incorporate a new idea in each report, whether that be a graphic illustration or a different kind of table or layout so as to inculcate innovation even in the reporting process.

Individual Development Needs

The ninth source of goals is individual development needs. One of the things that I mention in Performance Management Training sessions is that all employees are not the same. Employees are similar in human dignity but differ in ambition, motivation, skill, interest, personality, attitude and many other elements that affect performance. To an organisation that has a basic grasp of human resources management and little experience in performance management, this is usually a statement that raises eyebrows among participants. Some managers try to make all their employees the same, to mold them to be like themselves. This is a wrong concept of performance management and of getting people to show their best efforts. Managers need to work with their current employees and understand their capabilities and skills. In doing so, a manager can support an employee in addressing a development area through an innovative idea, a project or even the duties stated in one's job description. This source of goals is directly related to one specific employee and is based on a manager's intimate knowledge of his employees. It is not generic and will rarely be applied in the same sense and context to more than one individual.

Developmental Opportunities

The tenth source of goals comes from developmental or learning opportunities. Since performance management is about bringing the best out in each employee, in order to serve the interests of the organisation you will come across some employees who have developmental or learning needs. To improve their performance to the expected or desired level, you need to develop their skills and fill those learning or performance gaps. You can do this by setting developmental goals whereby you agree with the employee on development needs and what they must accomplish to bridge those gaps.

In addition to this one-on-one work, many organisations have what are called "mandatory learning events." These refer to specific and usually company- or industry-specific training activities or hours that an employee needs to have in order to meet performance expectations. An organisation may, for example, prescribe that all employees must complete fifty learning hours a year, five of which should be through e-learning. It can also be decided that all employees need to complete ethics or risk management training, and that failure to complete the same will result in an automatic downgrading of the employee's performance score. This area sometimes begs the question of whether the effort of learning or the learning outcome should be assessed. It is therefore important to recognise that performance management seeks to develop employees so long as that development is in support of achieving greater organisational objectives or does not detract from the attainment of set goals. Should an employee be rewarded for engaging in self-development learning or training? Or should the employee be penalized for not affording himself to a learning opportunity for which an organisation's financial and other resources have already been committed? The answer to these questions depends a lot on the organisation's performance management philosophy as well as on the reason for putting in place a performance management system. If the reason is to reward employees, their penalty is automatic when they do not attend a training session; if the reason is to develop employees, make sure they know they are the main beneficiaries and should take advantage of the opportunity.

The Departmental Objectives

The departments or units' objective is the eleventh source of goals. Each department is established to support the organisation in achieving its overall objectives—from manufacturing to procurement; from sales to finance and human resources management to marketing. All departments have a purpose and a mission. A common practice is for departments to craft their individual strategies in alignment with the overall organisational strategy. The strategy so developed is then broken down to goals and objectives, which are assigned to employees. Top management defines the goals for the organisation. Other levels of management interpret the goals for their departments and then set goals or objectives specific for their units. Then they develop plans or identify the activities required to accomplish the objectives and define the measures of success. Outcomes are the results that occur after having engaged in activities to meet the goals and objectives. An outcome is successful or not based on the measures that were used as shown in the figure below.

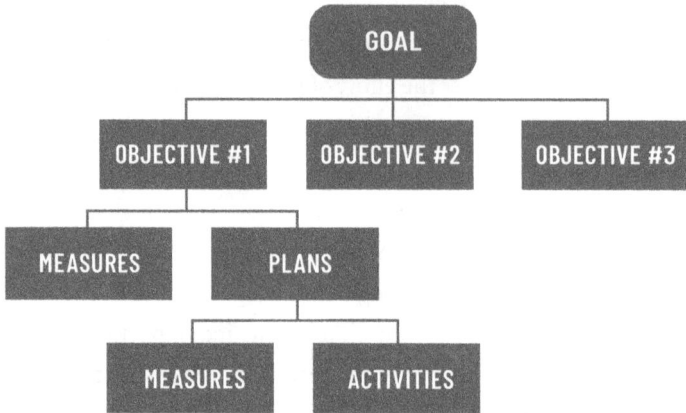

As I mentioned in the opening of this chapter, you need to judiciously apply yourself and your understanding of the current performance and capability of the employee when selecting which goals most align with the expectations of the organisation and with the employee's development needs. You should therefore not focus on using all the goals all the time. It should also be noted that the sources of goals and the role of the manager does not suggest that the manager will be the one setting the goals for the employee, but rather that the manager will prepare sample goals which will be discussed with each employee during the goal-setting meeting or the performance-contracting phase of the performance calendar. This is important so as to steer the conversation in the right direction as well as to have reference to higher-level goals at the departmental or unit position.

The employee will also have been provided with an opportunity to prepare his own goals to be discussed at the meeting. Managers can use a checklist such as the one shown below to ensure that all sources of goals have been evaluated and those that are relevant for the current performance period or a specific employee have been utilised. The checklist is a guide to assist the manager in goal setting, and I do not suggest that every item should correspond to a goal. There is in fact a useful way of combining goals to ensure that all dimensions are addressed. Those dimensions that are not addressed in the current performance period can then be the areas of focus during the next or subsequent performance period.

SOURCE	RELEVANT IN CURRENT EMPLOYEE SITUATION?	
1. Company strategy	YES	NO
2. Job description		
3. Targets		
4. Problem-solving issues		
5. Projects		
6. Behavioural expectations		
7. Organisational Values		
8. Innovative ideas		
9. Individual development needs		
10. Developmental opportunities		
11. Department's objectives		

From the above template it is possible to have employees in a department working on a combination of goals, each related to the above sources. While no single employee will have a goal from each source, the sources will all be represented in employee goals within a department. In addition, even for employees who carry out similar types of roles, there will be similar sources but differences due to the individual nature of the goal-setting process and also because of the actual difference in individuals in terms of past performance, ideals and capability. During the goal-setting meeting, the conversation should focus on the ideas and themes brought to the meeting. There is a lot of value to be derived from this conversation, as employees offer suggestions or different approaches they think they can use in order to achieve the departmental objectives.

Agree on SMART Goals

The next step is to agree upon goals that are SMART: specific, measurable, achievable, relevant and time bound. In a computerised performance management system both the manager and the employee will have documented their separate sets of goals for the employee to focus on in the computerised system. If this step is not computerised both the manager and the employee will come to the goal-setting meeting with their notes.

During the conversation the employee might want to carry out a different set of tasks than they currently do. The discussion on these tasks should continue if the tasks are within the mandate of the department (aligned); have a desirable outcome (specific); can be measured (measurable); are challenging and realistic given the time, resources and the employee's capability and development plan (relevant); and have deliverables that will be achieved during the current performance period (time bound). This step of jointly agreeing on performance goals is an element of shared decision-making. *Shared decision-making* (SDM) takes place when a corporate decision is made or at least influenced by more than one individual or group. SDM is a form of corporate democracy. If applied responsibly, such as in performance management goal setting and review, shared decision-making can boost the quality of decisions and increase the understanding, acceptance and support of those decisions. If staff and stakeholders are engaged in the decision-making process in some way, they are less likely to resist change and are more likely to embrace it as active and enthusiastic partners and not as reluctant followers. Shared decision-making can save time, money and other resources, and can advance the organisation towards its goals.

Create a Formal Document

The last thing to do in the goal-setting meeting is to create a final document that lists the goals that have been agreed upon by both manager and employee. This list will form the basis of the subsequent performance discussions and reviews. It will provide a road map for future discussions with the employee about their progress and performance. The document produced is variously referred to as a *performance plan*, a *performance agreement* or a *performance contract*. This document is typically prepared and stored on a digital platform.

The SMART goals so developed play an important role in managing the employees and motivating them to achieve more and do more. SMART goals help and motivate employees in the following ways:

1. **Goals give employees direction.**

   When you have a goal of reducing shipment of defective products by 5 percent by October, you know that you should direct your energy towards defects. The goal tells you what to focus on. For this reason, goals should be set carefully. Giving employees goals that are not aligned with company goals will be a problem, because goals will direct employees' energies to a certain end.

2. **Goals energise and tell employees not to stop until the goal is accomplished.**

   If you set goals for yourself such as "I will have a break from reading this book when I finish reading this section," you will not give up until you reach the end of the section. Even if you feel tired along the way, having this specific goal will urge you to move forward. The same thing happens when employees are energised on accomplishing their work in line with the set goals.

3. **Goals provide a challenge.**

   When people have goals and proceed to reach them, they feel a sense of accomplishment. This implies that the goals themselves are stretch goals and that they have not been achieved accidentally or by chance. Goals provide a challenge when they provide an individual with the ability to do something they previously thought was unachievable.

4. **SMART goals urge employees to think outside the box and rethink how they are working.**

   If the goal is not very difficult, it only motivates people to work faster or longer. If a goal is substantially difficult, merely working faster or longer will not get you the results. Instead, you will need to rethink the way you usually work and devise a creative way of working. It has been argued that this method resulted in designers and engineers in Japan inventing the bullet train. Having a goal that went beyond the speed capabilities of traditional trains prevented engineers from making minor improvements and inspired them to come up with a radically different concept.

5. **Goals let employees know what is expected of them.**

   How often do we hear employees say at the end of the year when they are being evaluated "I did not know" or "I wish you had told me"? Managers at times make assumptions that what is obvious to them is also obvious to the employee. Instead of making these assumptions, managers should spell out what it is that they expect of the employee so that they both know what is expected. This should not be done only once during the goal-setting step but should continue throughout the performance cycle.

6. **Goals let employees take responsibility for their performance.**

   Once an employee knows what is expected of him, he will look for ways and means to meet the expectations. This attitude of looking for the appropriate means to achieve performance expectations demonstrates an attitude that the employee is taking responsibility for his performance. If on the other hand an employee waits for perfect conditions or for people to act in a certain way or for the environment to be favourable, that individual is not taking responsibility for his performance but rather is waiting for things to fall into place through some magical force.

7. **Goals help employees see where their goals support organisational objectives.**

When a manager and employee collaborate in setting the employees performance goals, that employee is able to see the relationship between achieving his goals and how that achievement supports the attainment of organisational objectives. They are able to see this because they picture how the attainment of organisational goals is a combination of individual efforts and results throughout the organisation including their own.

8. **Goals direct efforts to focus on the unit's success.**

We saw that employees are not equal, and neither is their contribution to the success of their units the same as one another. One employee can do the work of three people, while another is very creative in the use of reusable components to develop new products. A manager needs to know the relative strengths and competencies of the employees he supervises in order to direct their efforts to the areas where they can produce the most value. This does not imply favouritism or lack of fairness but is a calculated move to allow everyone to do his or her best while focusing on the unit's success. This does not exclude the fact that managers will also expose employees in areas where they are not as strong as others with a view to developing them. These efforts at developing employees should not be carried out at the expense of achieving success in one's unit.

9. **Goals help employees keep track of how they are doing.**

Every employee would like to see growth and development in his career. That growth and development comes from the ability of the employee to consistently meet and exceed the performance expectations. In order to do this, managers must set goals with their employees that allow the employees to know how they are faring in the achievement of the agreed goals. Such a discussion also focuses on the challenges that employees are facing in achieving their goals and what they can do to improve performance.

10. **Goals help employees feel that their performance evaluations have an objective basis.**

If goals have not been set collaboratively with the employees, there will be a perception among the employees that their performance evaluations are biased. Such a perception may lead to disruptions in the workplace, thus reducing the amount of energy available for focusing on productive work.

11. **Goals allow employees to receive recognition for their accomplishments.**

One of the concerns managers and employees have when handling accomplishments relates to rewards. Some managers believe that if an employee carries out what was expected and does it at the right level of performance he is not due for a reward because he has simply achieved the set goals. If, however, the employee exceeds the goal expectations they become eligible to receive rewards. It needs to be clear from the onset to both manager and employee what accomplishments necessitate rewards and which ones don't. A discussion on rewards and recognition is found in the rewards and recognition chapter.

Case Study 3: Brandwagon Consultant's Aggressive Goals

A few years ago, a group of executives working in a global consultancy company, Brandwagon, in response to demands from their overseas headquarters decided to launch an aggressive growth initiative, which would more than triple its revenue in five years. They wanted to grow their top-line revenue to $200 million by the set year. In doing so, executives formulated targets in form of revenue goals for each of the business units. As the revenue targets were large, they were faced with a lot of skepticism and even resentment from a large portion of the workforce. Some of the skepticism even came from large business units who felt that there were recipients of directives from people not in tune with the local business environment.

When the executives noticed this passive resistance, they scaled down the goals slightly, but the resistance did not fade. The organisation went ahead to develop key performance criteria and assigned these to the business units who were in turn told to cascade the same to their managers and so on.

The process was muddled with a lot of confusion, and at the end of the first year the targets were not achieved but the shortfalls were rolled on to the following year with an added percentage increment. Managers and staff found that they could not receive the bonuses they were previously accustomed to receiving, as the targets became moving targets. Business unit leaders and staff were not consulted on the goals, nor were their opinions sought on how feasible the goals were. Suffice it to say that the five-year revenue growth goals were not achieved.

Setting aggressive goals and targets is good business practice; however, this should be done based on the willingness to support people in meeting their performance targets, and to get them enthused about taking action to meet these goals. Employees also need to see what is in it for them through the alignment between their personal goals and those of the organisation.

CHAPTER 3

REVIEWS THAT FOSTER ACHIEVEMENT

"Administration must be flawless; HR practices must be innovative and integrated; and HR must turn strategic aspirations into HR actions."
—DAVID ULRICH, the Father of Modern Human Resources Management

PERFORMANCE REVIEWS ARE ONE OF the most dreaded roles by managers. They instill some fear among both managers and employees, which in turn tends to render reviews less useful in achieving the intended objectives. One of the keys to addressing this fear and unease is open discussions between the manager and the subordinate about the performance appraisal process, its frequency and its outputs. I am a strong advocate for managers to undergo continual training on how to carry out unbiased reviews and to provide co-coaching opportunities for each other to practice review techniques in a supportive environment.

Quality of Performance Tools

The performance appraisal form is one of the tools used in the management of performance. The form must be designed in such a way that it possesses the desired qualities. One of these is relevance. *Relevance* is defined as the degree to which the rating form includes necessary information. The tool might have *criterion deficiency* in which pertinent performance criteria are omitted, or *criterion contamination* which entails the inclusion of irrelevant criteria on the rating form.

The second quality of a good performance appraisal form is the definition of clear performance standards. Clear performance standards indicate the level of performance that an employee is expected to achieve. They also help direct employee behaviour and help supervisors provide more accurate ratings.

Some managers believe that providing clear performance standards to an employee is like setting an examination and providing the marking scheme with it to examination takers. This is incorrect firstly because in business there are usually multiple approaches to achieving set objectives, and secondly because employee performance is not a test of right or wrong but of creatively applying oneself to achieving targets even if the method used might be different from that of the supervisor.

The third quality is accuracy of the ratings. Accurate ratings reflect the employees' actual job performance levels while inaccuracy in ratings is most often attributable to the presence of rater errors.

Use a Handbook

A performance management handbook is a short guide that HR departments prepare for managers to help in their performance management roles. The handbook typically describes the generic and specific elements of the performance management system. In one organisation this guidebook was created and filed in a spring file so that each time a page or section changed the manager had to remove only the changed pages from his spring file and replace them with the new content. Training offered in such cases would center around the changed contents. Is it possible to effectively manage performance without providing managers with handbooks? I would answer that it is as easy to do as it is to operate a factory or assembly line without manuals. The experienced manager may easily cope with the role without referring to the manual; however, new managers will find it hard to fully come to terms with the requirements of the performance management system.

On joining an organisation, every new manager should receive this handbook and induction sessions should include a session on performance management with breakaway sessions for employees who do not have supervisory authority and for those who do have supervisory responsibility. The aim of doing this is for all to be aware of their respective roles as defined in the performance management handbook. The handbook might also contain other tools such as planning and goal-cascading tools, conversation and feedback-giving tools, and discrepancy-resolution tools in the manager and employee self-assessments.

A coaching handbook is another form of performance support that managers who are preferably trained in coaching should have access to. The coaching handbook helps the manager carry out coaching in an effective way. This handbook can also contain a number of coaching scenarios which would provide guidance to the manager on how to handle similar cases that they experience. It does this by developing new ways of thinking, feeling, acting, learning, leading and relating to others so as to build individual and organisational effectiveness.

Job Aids

Job aids are an additional tool in the manager's performance arsenal. Job aids are quick reference devices designed to direct or guide someone in the execution of a task. They contain information that prompts people to act in specific ways. Job aids are part of everyday life—for example, a computer software help screen, the grocery list you create for yourself, the troubleshooting steps on the inside lid of the washing machine, and the instructions that come with a piece of equipment on how to assemble or install it are all job aids. Job aids can be as simple as sticky notes attached to a computer or wall to remind you of information you might otherwise forget. They may use words, graphics, symbols and colors; be electronic or in a printed format; and be permanently affixed to the site where they are needed or portable. The important thing is for an aid to be accessible when needed and use commonly understood symbols and terms.

When a task is dangerous or presents a lot of risk to people or assets (for example, landing an airplane), the use of job aids is required and built into the job; it is an expected way to do business. When the goal is to prevent errors, organisations seek ways to automate the task or design systems that limit people's decisions and prescribe a sequence of steps, like computerised data-entry screens that accept only alpha or numeric symbols of predetermined lengths. Despite the growing use of electronic aids to guide people's decisions, job aids are still underutilised as tools to help people be more exact and efficient. Job aids related to performance reviews should be widely promoted and used.

Rating Scales

There are frequent discussions on rating scales, with some organisations even opting to eliminate the use of rating scales; these organisations argue that assigning a number or grade to an employee does not give justice to the human person or even capture all aspects of work undertaken throughout the year. There are three types of rating scales: performance based, normative based and frequency based. The performance-based scales will usually include statements such as *meets expectations* or *exceeds expectations*, while normative-based scales will use words such as *average* or *above average*. In the case of frequency-based scales the words *always* or *sometimes* are used.

The choice of which type of scale to use depends on the nature of the work as well as the behavioural competencies. I recall discussions with a senior executive who used to argue that one cannot exceed expectations in certain values such as integrity. This, he argued, was because you either had integrity or not. What are the degrees of integrity, and how can one create its performance levels?

Additionally, the scales can use multiple levels such as a five-point rating system in which the performance dimension is defined according to the behaviours exhibited and their frequency.

Dimension Rating

5: Consistently exceeds requirements, no improvements needed

4: Exceeds most requirements

3: Usually meets requirements, acceptable performance

2: Usually meets most requirements, but needs much improvement

1: Does not meet minimum requirements, needs immediate and extensive improvement

In using such a formula, managers need to get into the habit of documenting behaviours observed rather than relying on memory. This is one case of the automation of performance management systems. The employee behaviour might, for example, consist of ten different aspects. The manager might observe eight of them, document four and recall two. If the recency error—in which a manager's appraisal is based on what he recalls—prevails, the employee will appear to have performed well or badly depending only on the facts or behaviours that the manager recalls; yet in this example there were ten different behavioural elements that should have been captured. We tend to remember first impressions, recent behaviours, unusual behaviours, extreme behaviours and behaviour that is consistent with our opinions. The performance management system should therefore seek to eliminate potential bias by giving an employee an opportunity to provide evidence relating to behaviours that the manager might not have observed or might have ignored through bias; the system should also ensure appropriate documentation is kept by all parties on a regular basis.

This further means that the performance review should not be an annual event but rather ongoing conversations between managers and subordinates such that, at the end of the performance period when it comes to "form filling," both parties will be on the same page as performance discussions have been held throughout the performance period. Employee performance records should contain information relating to critical incidents, which are examples of poor or excellent behaviour. This information should also include examples. In order to address performance gaps in a timely fashion, organisations should carry out semiannual reviews. The key challenge faced in organisations which hold semiannual reviews is the consistency and rigour with which they are carried out. In many cases the review timetable is not observed, and the quality of the reviews is of a lower standard compared to end-of-year appraisals. In order to give more meaning to the semiannual review process, managers should get into the habit of documenting performance evidence and also establishing frequent touch points with their staff in order to discuss any performance concerns or give recognition and compliments. I am a strong proponent of quarterly formal reviews.

In order to eliminate rating errors such as the central-tendency error—in which employees tend to be appraised at the middle of the scale—some organisations opt for a four-point scale, which forces the manager to provide a rating based on the portfolio of evidence in his possession.

Such a four-point scale could resemble the one shown below:

4: Exceptional performance in which an employee meets over 120 percent of the assigned performance goals

3: High performance in which an employee meets over 100 percent of the assigned performance goals

2: Good performance in which an employee meets all assigned performance goals

1: Low performance in which an employee meets less than 75 percent of the assigned performance goals

Sources of Feedback

Employees are often assessed based on the feedback that their supervisors or line managers provide. Sometimes organisations use a variety of sources to determine the feedback and appraisal comments to be provided to employees. These sources have their benefits and drawbacks, and the evolution of the performance management system should seek to limit or curtail weaknesses while promoting the positive elements of each source.

SOURCE	ADVANTAGES	POTENTIAL DRAWBACKS
Supervisory ratings	• Serve as management tools for supervisor • Give supervisors a means to direct and monitor employee behaviour	• Supervisor's bias might limit objectivity • Supervisor might not get along with a given employee or employee segment
Peer ratings	• Supplement supervisory ratings • Help develop a consensus about an individual's performance • Help eliminate biases and lead to greater employee acceptance of appraisal systems	• Peers might not understand the competencies that the employee lacks or needs • Peers might be influenced • Peers might not have a full understanding of the strategy of the department or the organisation • Can be misused to skew the reward system • Friendship and social relations limit the usefulness of peer ratings
Self ratings	• Useful in employee development	• Employees can be biased, only seeing the positives in their behaviours
Customer ratings	• Provide additional dimensions on areas of employee performance • Not subject to debate or questioning	• Might not be structured effectively • Might not be linked to the department's or organisation's objectives • Hard to attribute customer feedback to a single individual in a team-based environment

In the gig economy, labour will not be employed on a full-time basis in any organisation. The success of a gig worker and how well he performs in one gig will determine his likelihood of getting the next gig. Organisations increasingly need to learn to integrate and leverage this part-time and contingent workforce in order to meet business needs. Operating effectively in the gig economy poses a number of questions. How can companies best use and schedule external staff to improve the productivity of their own workers and increase profitability? How can companies leverage contingent workers to access some of the most talented and highly skilled people in the workforce? The remuneration of gig workers should be carefully studied, as full-time staff will tend to compare their own remuneration and performance with that of gig workers and may opt for the latter if they feel that it is more attractive. This shift could have implications on the consistent implementation of an organisation's strategy and even the time it takes to onboard employees and get them ready for the tasks that lie ahead. Gig workers themselves must be reviewed so they have tenable references to take with them to their next gig.

Review Frequency and Process

My experience has taught me that a review carried out once a year without any corresponding performance discussions in the middle of the year is as good as no review. This is because there are too many highs and lows that occur during the year to be able to capture them in a single review period and give them the importance they deserve. Employees are uneasy discussing their performance over a one-year period, especially if they do not have their own performance documented in a structured manner. Many organisations carry out two formal reviews: one in the middle of the year and one at the end of the year. These two reviews are usually complemented by periodic informal reviews.

Once the frequency of reviews has been determined, it is good practice to ensure consistency in the format of the review meeting so that all employees in the organisation experience the process in a similar manner. The review process will take the following steps:

Step One: Preparation

- Before the meeting, the manager or supervisor should ask the team member to prepare for the meeting by considering how they have performed against the agreed period goals.

- While the employee is preparing for the meeting, you as the manager or reviewer should also prepare by reviewing your notes and the record of your previous review meeting. You ought to be clear on your core messages, as people rarely hear everything you say, particularly when they are feeling uncomfortable. Capture your core message in one or two sentences. Practice saying them, and if possible, gain feedback on their impact.

Step Two: Agree the Agenda

- At the start of the meeting, spend a little time welcoming the employee and making them feel as comfortable as possible.

- Outline the process that the meeting will follow.

Step Three: Evaluate Past and Present Performance

- Ask them first how they would describe their performance in the period under review.

- Ask questions to clarify your understanding of their viewpoint, particularly if it is at odds with yours.

- Review the performance review form and record past behaviours and incidents that have impacted performance.

Step Four: Discuss Ideas for Development/Action Plan

- Find out what goals and plans the employee has for their career.

- Discover if the employee's plans and the company's plans are in alignment or differ.

- Talk about the skills and experience needed for the employee to accomplish their career goals.

Step Five: Agree upon Specific Steps to be Taken by Both Parties

- Create a to-do list for you as the manager; have the employee create his own to-do list.
  - The lists do not have to be long, and they do not have to contain an equal number of items. The goal is to have a written action plan that is achievable and valuable to both parties—including deadlines.

Step Six: Summarise the Performance Review Meeting and Express Support

- Wrap up the conversation by recapping the key discussion points.

- Thank the employee for their participation, and show your support for the employee.

- Ask the employee to give you some feedback. Find out if you're providing valuable support. Ask for suggestions on ways you can improve as a manager.

Step Seven: Document Agreed Actions and Outcomes

- Create a list of agreed actions that both you as the manager or supervisor and the employee will take in order to address performance gaps.

- Set realistic deadlines for carrying out the agreed actions.

- Highlight areas that are going well and areas that the employee needs to improve in.

- Suggest a date for the next one-on-one session to follow up on progress made in the interim.

Enhancing Objectivity in the Review Process

There are a number of methods that are used to support managers being more objective in the review process. These include training, coaching and use of performance support tools such as handbooks. Managers should be aware of a number of rating errors which might cloud their judgment and limit objectivity. These are:

- **Leniency error:** In this case raters provide ratings that are unduly high.

- **Severity error:** In this case ratings are unduly low. The severity and leniency errors arise from political reasons, raters' lack of conscientiousness and personal biases.

- **Central-tendency error:** In this case appraisers purposely avoid giving extreme ratings even when such ratings are warranted. The causes of central-tendency errors are poor administrative procedures and rating scale end points which are unrealistically defined.

- **Halo effect:** In this case the appraiser's overall impression of an employee is based on a particular characteristic. This acts as a barrier to accurate appraisals and is caused by vague rating standards and failure to conscientiously complete the rating form.

- **Implicit personality theory:** In this case the rater's estimation of an employee's performance is based on a trait that is related to the occurrence of another trait or feature; this affects how different types of people behave in certain situations. A rater might, for example, associate quietness with laziness or strictness with coldheartedness. Using this theory, organisations are unable to identify employees' specific strengths and weaknesses.

- **Recency error:** In this case ratings are heavily influenced by recent events that are more easily remembered. Ratings that unduly reflect recent events can present a false picture of the individual's job performance during the entire rating period.

- **Similar-to-me error:** In this case a rater gives higher ratings to employees with certain attributes similar to his (e.g., values, habits, lifestyle and such attributes).

- **Contrast effect:** This involves direct comparison and rating of a staff member to others at the same or higher levels, rather than against the performance on goals. It compares individuals with each other rather than comparing individuals with the performance standards.

Another way of enhancing objectivity in the review process is the use of calibration or performance moderation. I recall an organisation that practiced performance moderation through the use of a committee. The committee was comprised of managers who had some input about an employee or who had worked with the said employee during the performance period. The managers came together to rationalise the performance evaluations and to ensure objectivity in the process as well as comparability within and among departments. It so happens that managers attending the moderation sessions would leak information out to employees, including details of the discussions which were supposed to be confidential. The result of this is that employees would feel disenfranchised as they felt they had no way of airing their own views. What's more, the organisation espoused a value they called integrity; yet managers who leaked information were not called upon to account for their actions.

Improving Self-Assessments

The practice of allowing employees to carry out an initial self-assessment is a good practice as it has the effect of reducing defensiveness, highlighting areas of disagreement with supervisors, and leading to improved job performance. Self-assessment can also help individuals identify weaknesses and contribute to self-learning. Feedback plays a crucial role in the self-assessment process, as it can provide direction for improved performance. Self-assessments can be effective and useful when the process utilises individual practice profiles and includes real-world performance; validating results externally and linking them to additional learning activities can cultivate further effectiveness of the assessments.

Different leadership styles can affect self-assessment by influencing how leaders interact with their subordinates and how they perceive themselves. Various leadership styles have been identified, including guiding, directing, participating, and delegating.

The lack of concordance between leaders and subordinates in self-evaluation can be influenced by factors such as culture, work environment and biases. It is important for leaders to focus on building strong interpersonal relationships, communication and trust to enhance their self-knowledge, confidence and decision-making abilities. Laisser-faire leaders affect self-assessment differently based on gender. Different leadership styles, such as transformational and participative leadership, can impact organisational success by influencing employee satisfaction and productivity. Generational differences in leadership styles, like the preference for honesty and communication, also play a role in organisational success. Employees respond more favorably to a transformational leadership style compared to an authoritative leadership style. Transformational leadership is recommended by supervisors as the most suitable form of leadership to improve employee performance. Authoritative leaders are described as controlling, power-oriented, and coercive, making decisions without input from subordinates. This type of leadership can lead to structure and compliance but may not consider feelings. Collaborative leadership, on the other hand, involves open-mindedness, inviting discussions and seeking consensus, which can lead to long term results and positive relationships.

Managers and executives should carefully understand their own and their employees' expectations of the review process and ensure that the process is designed to address the respective aspirations and expectations while eliminating all forms of subjectivity.

CHAPTER 4

THE FORMAT OF PERFORMANCE EXPECTATIONS

"Without credible communication, and a lot of it, employees' hearts and minds are never captured."
—JOHN KOTTER

A NEW EMPLOYEE JOINS AN organisation and attends the induction sessions that have been planned and is then sent back to the department for which he has been hired to go and carry out his duties. There is a belief that the induction session is enough to ground employees in what they need to do within the organisation. Experience has shown that this is hardly enough, for after the employee has attended the induction session, he tends to engage in discussions with fellow employees about how things are done in the particular organisation. The employee is not only told where he can go for his meals and breaks but is also socialised on the different personalities within the organisation. He is told who to fear, who to respect and who he should make friends with in order to enhance his career. If the employee happens to join the organisation in between the performance periods he is at a major disadvantage because most managers do not make time to scale performance expectations according to the number of months, days or weeks left in the performance period. If in fact there are a number of weeks or days left, most managers leave the activity of goal setting and communicating expectations to the next performance period. One wonders why the employee had to be onboarded if there was no need that had to be addressed within those remaining days, weeks or months. Any employee who joins an organisation needs to understand the expectations of the executives, customers, stakeholders and hiring manager in order to be effective in his role.

Encouraging and fostering a performance culture or performance management practices in an organisation goes beyond the appraisal period and deals with work that is carried out on a day-to-day basis. When a manager assigns work or a task to an employee, he needs also to specify the performance standards in terms of work standards and a time frame in which things must be completed. These expectations need to be communicated before the task is started, and an opportunity must be provided to the employee to ask questions or clarify issues. It is very easy for an individual to assume that saying one thing and understanding it in one's mind is equivalent to the same thing being understood the same way by the person hearing you. People hear and interpret messages differently. The elements of the performance management system need to be communicated and explained even if the employee is not new to the organisation. A change in goals or measures needs to be clearly stated with a basis for the change made. Talking is not the same as communicating.

To most individuals, the format of a performance management system is the actual appraisal form and the ratings contained therein. These two elements are important because the form should be well designed in order to make it easy to use, and the ratings should allow for objectivity in the process. There is a belief that automating the performance management system will make it more objective and improve acceptability of the results of evaluation. This is not accurate as there are many performance management systems that are not computerised but which are much more fair and objective than the ones that are. Remember the age-old computer adage: garbage-in, garbage-out!

Common Managerial Assumptions

Here are some common mistakes managers and supervisors make in failing to communicate expectations:

1. They assume that people know what they are supposed to produce and for whom.

2. They assume people understand on what basis their performance will be measured.

3. They assume that what is being measured drives the appropriate behaviours and generates the desired results.

4. They believe everyone knows and agrees on the criteria to be used to judge whether or not the work is of sufficient quantity, quality and timeliness to be of value to those who depend on it.

5. They fail to communicate what is expected in terms of performance and confirm that the communication was understood.

For most individuals, job descriptions and hiring criteria begin the process of defining and communicating expectations. People expect their job descriptions to be accurate. When people are hired and discover that what is expected is significantly different from what they first understood about the job, they become confused and the organisation risks not getting the level of performance it requires. Therefore, you should find out what information is contained in the job description and confirm that your supervisors set appropriate expectations. Unfortunately, some job descriptions do not specify objectives, deliverables or measures. Instead, HR usually expects the manager to communicate what the objectives, deliverables and measures are. Sometimes it helps just to ask why the organisation even created your unit and the job positions in it. There must have been an expectation that something would be better accomplished or different by having your work unit and the job positions within it.

Know Your "Why"

It can help you as a manager or supervisor to confirm your understanding of who your customers are and who depends on or benefits from your unit's outputs. Knowing why you exist and who relies on the work you produce helps you to determine what your unit's objectives are. The assumption is that the objectives were derived from the goals of the department or division; however, department goals are not always easy to translate into objectives for smaller work units or individuals. Knowing who your customers are can add clarity and purpose.

Managers and supervisors often overlook the importance of periodically questioning just what their deliverables are and who depends on them. It is easier for people who directly interface with external customers, such as sales, or for those who manufacture goods to understand what they do and for whom. People in other types of jobs may feel they are too removed from top management or customers and lack sight of their roles in the organisation. The concept of an internal customer is also not readily understood, because people do not always see their work as being part of a larger process. Yet being clear about your deliverables and customers is essential to evaluating your people's performance, improving your work processes and acting as a champion for your group.

To reconfirm just what your group's deliverables are, start by asking who your customers are. Next, ask what your group produces that those customers rely on; what do customers require of your group to meet their needs or to do their work? Include physical items, information and emotional factors. Emotional deliverables include a sense of confidence and due diligence, especially if your group performs an audit or quality assurance function.

Communicate Performance Expectations

When communicating performance expectations, a manager has to have the following objectives in mind:

- To build awareness of the performance goals and metrics at all levels of the organisation and department.

- To provide education on key performance concepts to all staff.

- To generate the engagement and commitment of staff in the process.

- To encourage staff participation in the process.

- To generate enthusiasm for performance management.

- To ensure team results are disseminated rapidly and effectively.

- To explain elements and sections of the performance contract document.

If expectations aren't communicated clearly, it can be detrimental to the success of your team. Many employees think that performance management is about performance appraisals, and they gear all their efforts towards ticking a box in line with the agreed formulation. This limited view of performance management that equates it with performance appraisal is based largely on the fact that bonuses, rewards and career growth prospects in many organisations are linked to the results of performance appraisals. Other elements of performance management such as improving organisational performance, fostering employee growth and cultivating motivation seem to be largely left out, while a lot of work and time is spent discussing whether or not employees have met stated performance goals. There is little discussion about whether employees have become better operational or managerial staff and how the organisation has benefited from their improved skills, capability and attitudes.

Rating Scale Drawbacks

One of the key elements of performance appraisals that causes a lot of problems is the rating scales that are used in many organisations. Some organisations use a five-point rating scale in which a score of one (1) means that an employee has not met their performance expectations while a score of five (5) means that an employee has exceeded their performance expectations by far. A score of three (3) means that an employee has met all performance objectives. Due to the nature of competition at work, today's employees strive to achieve a rating of 4 or 5, which is largely not attainable by the majority of the employees. Only a few employees can achieve a rating of 4 or 5. This is attributable largely to the nature of work that the employees carry out as well as the uniqueness of employees. In a target-based working environment it is possible to have employees who achieve ratings of 4 or 5, but in an operations environment, it becomes harder to have such ratings.

In working with a banking client, a senior official in the procurement department walked to me during one of the breaks and told me that he found in his department it was hard to give ratings of 4 or 5 because the employees were largely carrying out their assigned tasks within the agreed timelines according to the set departmental plan. The employees themselves would feel that their work deserved more than a rating of 3 because of how important the work was, but they were unable to justify a higher rating, even on the basis of having worked in the same organisation for a long period of time. Employees in organisations need to be aware of this reality, while managers should clearly communicate what the different rating scales mean. Managers too should be aware of the error of central tendency in which they rate all or most employees at the level of 3 in order to minimize complaints, even when the performance of employees might deserve more or less.

A purpose-driven organisation shows its consumers and employees that it takes purpose seriously by actively demonstrating the steps it's taking to meet this promise. People are more willing and motivated to complete assigned tasks if they can relate them to something with meaning. An employee's task should not be viewed in isolation but in conjunction with its contribution to the wider team, department and organisation at large.

Employees should be encouraged to come to the goal-setting meeting with a notepad and pen. It is good practice when assigning bigger tasks or projects to employees to encourage them to write down what is expected of them, including a breakdown of steps of actions needed in order to achieve the goal. This practice helps the employee commit to the goal and ensures that both the manager and the employee are on the same page. It also provides a basis for follow-up and reviewing progress or even carrying out corrective action. If the agreed plan is not clear, it becomes harder to accomplish with the passage of time. There are various other tools that you can use to keep track of agreed goals and the progress being made.

Performance Coaching Tips

The following tips are useful when communicating anticipated performance:

1. **Solidify your expectations**

   As you assign a task, you need to make it clear that you require a high standard of work completed and the time frame in which it must be done. You should not be ambiguous when it comes to what you're asking of people: make things clear from the outset and ensure that people know what to do if they have issues or questions; if, for example, they should be checking in or addressing queries with their team lead, or with you as a manager directly. Some managers think that if they solidify their expectations, they make it easier for the employee to achieve superior results without expending much effort or thought. This is incorrect because well-communicated performance expectations reduce the need for rework and correcting errors once the performance cycle has started. Such solidly communicated expectations are indeed in the interest of both manager and employee and should align to the organisational and stakeholder objectives of achieving superior results.

2. Give a purpose

People will be far more willing and motivated to complete what is expected of them if they can relate it to something with meaning. Instead of just asking people to complete a specific report, for example, share with them what that report will accomplish on a larger scale; how it will contribute in conjunction with the work of the rest of the team, and how it will positively impact the organisation in a wider sense. Simon Sinek argues that you should always begin with the "why" because then you are communicating directly to the person's heart. Purposeful communication and purposeful intent make it much easier for the employee to not only work from his heart but also to relate his work to the team and to the wider organisational interests.

3. Confirm steps

It's good practice when assigning bigger tasks or projects to encourage people to write down what's expected of them with a breakdown of steps or actions needed in order to achieve the goal. This is not only helpful in the sense that it will help people commit to and be motivated to complete goals, but it also further ensures you remain on the same page and have a solid plan of action moving forward. There are various tools you can use to keep track of goals and the progress being made. It is not uncommon for a manager to summarise the information on how the task will be accomplished and to request the employee to describe his own understanding of the task steps and deliverables.

4. Check back

You should casually check back with the employee after a few days to reconfirm that the assigned tasks are proceeding as agreed. There is a fine line between keeping people on task and micromanaging, and it's important to acknowledge this. It's not necessary to be on people's backs constantly. The key is to casually check in with people to ensure expectations are being met. Taking ten minutes to converse over coffee and asking if your staff is on track to meet expectations is a simple and effective way of checking back. You can also ask your employees if they feel that the agreed deadlines are still realistic. This will not only mean that both you and your staff are on the same page and concerns can be addressed, but it also shows people that you are invested in them and what they're doing and want to take the time out to discuss it.

5. Hold regular meetings

As part of setting expectations it is important to agree with staff on follow-up schedules. You should have regular, perhaps bimonthly, meetings with the team to keep a two-way conversation flowing and ensure that communicating what you want isn't just something which happens when you assign tasks or projects. Set clear goals during these meetings for the team, and break them down into goals for individuals so that everyone knows both exactly what they are working towards and the practical steps to get there.

6. Hold one-on-ones

Having solo conversations around progress can keep you on the same page as your team and make sure that once initial expectations have been set, the conversation remains open and the opportunity for any discussion needed is there. One-on-ones can be helpful to your own growth, as it's not just your team that can gain feedback—it's also a great opportunity for you to grow as a manager or an executive; you can tailor how you interact with people once you know them on a more personal level and are aware of how they prefer things communicated to them, whether it's being assigned a task, setting goals or having a general performance-based conversation.

Process rigour, which is the strict adherence to standards, in communication is key to meeting expectations successfully. Additionally, planning ahead on timelines to engage employees and setting expectations with constructive and ongoing dialogues during such engagement will lead to greater success in employees meeting expectations. A clear process in time-line and communication will remove the element of surprise and result in a productive engagement. Usually the human resources department is the custodian of process rigour, while supervisors observe the process and have the responsibilities to communicate, translate changing business/peo-ple dynamics to employees and continually create a strong line-of-sight be-tween changing business context and performance expectations. With the rise of human resource business partnering, line managers have additional support in the form of frequent interaction with their respective business partner.

Aligning Communications to Management Expectations

While communicating expectations to your staff, it is important to align what you communicate to the expectations of top management.

Top management communicates what is important by:

- What is and is not mentioned publicly, during briefings, meetings and announcements

- Who is left out, not invited or not given time to speak at meetings

- The order in which topics are addressed

- The amount of time, money and talent committed to an issue

Top management begins the process of providing direction when it establishes the goals for the year. Next, middle management provides di-rection for first-line managers and supervisors by setting department goals based on its interpretation of top management's messages and behaviour. Finally, first-line managers and supervisors provide direction for their work units based on their interpretation of their management's behaviour and messages. This trickle-down process only works when the goals that are communicated are congruent with what management pays attention to and with what gets measured, and if what gets measured supports the intended results.

Therefore, leaders provide direction in what they attend to and what they measure, not necessarily by what they say are the goals. However, what gets their attention and is measured should be consistent with what they said were the goals. Unfortunately, this does not always happen. Worse still, compensation and bonus plans do not always support what the company says it wants its people to accomplish. As a result, some companies are now basing a portion of managers' bonuses on the performance of the work unit over more than one year and have even extended the performance period to twenty-four to thirty-six months. This sends an especially strong message if the manager is on a rotational assignment, makes some change, or implements an initiative and then goes on to the next assignment, never to experience the impact of his or her decisions. Such a goal could include saving the company a percentage amount of money as part of ongoing cost-cutting initiatives in a company.

Statements are made in meetings and on the fly. Some of those statements come from top management "thinking out loud," and others are merely wish lists but are expressed like rules or goals. The onus is on you, the manager, to interpret what you heard or have been told, decide how much latitude you really have and figure out how to reframe the message in a way that better reflects the intent. Do you honour the spirit of the statement or its literal meaning? Sometimes honouring the literal statement can be malicious obedience, especially if you know it's not in the best interest of the organisation. An executive in a meeting can say that the organisation is in the process of acquiring a competitor. Acquisitions, as we know, do not always turn out as planned. It is therefore imperative for the manager who hears this utterance and has a view to creating a performance plan to create realistic objectives and not be attracted by the novelty of an acquisition which may not even occur in the current period.

People shape their behaviour based on what they see management attending to and by what is counted. Top management's job is to assure that what they pay attention to and measure gives them an accurate understanding of how well the organisation is doing. Your job as a manager or supervisor is to transform what the organisation measures into criteria that make sense for your work unit and can be tracked. Human performance depends on the goals and measures being aligned; otherwise there is confusion and the misdirection of resources.

What you measure usually comes from:

- The goals and objectives of the work unit and individuals for the year or for a specific assignment

- Your and your unit's deliverables or outputs

- Your customers' (internal and external) expectations of you and your group

- Your own interest in evaluating someone's performance, perhaps to identify development needs, performance issues or promotional readiness

Typically, managers and supervisors measure the quantity, quality, timeliness, and accuracy of the work produced and the results that ensue. However, you must decide why you want to measure and communicate this to your staff. It could be that you want to know more about the proficiency, productivity or performance of your unit, specific individuals or a new process you put in place. Whatever the reason, you should decide on the questions you want to answer through the process of measuring. For example, do you want to confirm that someone knows, can do or is doing something or that he or she gets along with others; that a new process saved time, reduced errors or reduced costs; or that customers are receiving what they want? Your questions lead you to an appropriate combination of measures.

The process in most organisations is for top management to communicate what it sees as the goals for the coming year and how they will be measured. It is especially important that the stated measures be congruent, be appropriate for the different business units and support the organisation's short-term and long-term goals. People notice when the information, behaviours and results that leaders attend to are not consistent with their original message. A leader who promotes a results-oriented working environment in his words but fails to take action on individuals who use unethical methods to achieve business results is setting up the organisation for failure. On the other hand, a leader who holds such individuals to account even if they are stellar performers creates an organisation in which everyone is valued and treated equally. At a minimum, leaders should repeatedly send the messages that reinforce the same goal, priorities and course of action. If the priorities change, leaders should acknowledge that the focus has changed. Leaders are seen as consistent when they reward behaviours and results that are congruent with what they said were the goals, keep the same issues on their agenda, and regularly ask about the status of work they had previously said was important. Consistency and congruency are what distinguish leadership from management.

It is your job to interpret and translate the policy, goals and measures so they are meaningful to the work group. You also have the job of giving top management feedback on the utility of their information. Therefore, make sure that what you pay attention to supports the organisation's goals and professed values. At the same time, you must help your superior stay focused on what makes sense over time. Therefore, in collaboration with coworkers, staff and your internal customers, you must do the following:

- Define the deliverable at whatever level is appropriate for you

- Specify what the expected and assumed outcome is

- Specify what aftereffects you want to avoid or have happen

- Identify the energy and resources that will be required to sustain the outcomes beyond the immediate period of time in question

Someone has to set expectations and decide what measures to use to judge whether or not those expectations were met. Measures are the criteria used to determine whether you are ahead or behind. The challenge is how to select measures that support the results you want and make sure in the process you don't accidentally encourage behaviours that are not in the best interest of the organisation. Alignment starts with being clear and in agreement on the objectives and deliverables of the job. Once this is clear you can begin to identify attributes that would indicate that the objectives are being accomplished in keeping with the organisation's goals and values.

Just as you take cues from top management as to what is important, your team does the same with you. They interpret what is important to you by the questions you ask, what you talk about, what you report to others, and what you measure. Therefore, it is important to be clear in your own mind about what you expect and what you will use as evidence of performance. Therefore, the act of communicating expectations is a fine balance between the expectations of your superiors, yourself, your customers, stakeholders and your employees. Each of these sets of expectations should be brought to the table, discussed and communicated effectively. As a manager you should also link the employee goals to the varied expectations by demonstrating how the work tasks meet the needs of the different stakeholders. This does not mean that you will set different goals for different stakeholder groups. In some cases you might have to do that, but in most cases aligning the employee goals to key stakeholders also has a way of ensuring that the needs of other linked or affiliated stakeholders are met. In meeting the needs of executives and customers, for example, the employee could also end up meeting the expectations of other stakeholders such as regulators and shareholders as well as the objectives and plans of the department or unit. You just need to be smart about how you do it, communicate it and monitor it as we shall see in the following chapters.

Case Study 4: Team Goals for Group Success

In working with teams, individuals have goals, which are dependent on the individual's mandate and on the team requirements at large. Teams also have other needs apart from those directly related to work performance, such as a sense of belonging and feeling valued. I used this idea to develop team roles that while promoting team spirit also contributed to a functioning team. These roles included social welfare, knowledge management and research. A few members were assigned to a sub-team which dealt with other issues; for example, three team members were assigned to the "social committee," and it was their role to ensure team happiness and take care of the social needs like birthdays of individual team members, team awaydays and coordinating the team's annual social calendar. While these tasks were not used for performance appraisal purposes, they not only contributed to an improvement in team morale but also in developing other skills of the sub-team such as event management, negotiation and emotional intelligence.

Setting performance expectations should be undertaken in a way that serves the development needs of the organisation, as well as helps further employees' unique skills in personal development.

CHAPTER 5

OPENNESS OF THE APPRAISAL SYSTEM

"We all need people who will give us feedback. That's how we improve."
—BILL GATES, Founder of Microsoft Corporation

CHARLES MWANGI WAS AN EXECUTIVE in a trading company in East Africa. He previously worked for many organisations, and throughout his working life he had been guided on the process of performance contracting and goal setting. When I met him in his current organisation he mentioned to me that he had not yet gone through a formal induction and that he hoped to receive a briefing of the strategy of the organisation and how the performance management system works so that he could be clear from the outset on what was required of him in his new role. A general induction or overview of the performance management system and framework is the first open proclamation that the organisation takes performance management seriously and that its elements are openly discussed and shared with new employees.

When employees join an organisation they have an expectation that their performance or any gaps in such performance should be known only by their immediate supervisor or sometimes also by the human resources department. Performance management and appraisal systems now tend to challenge this expectation because organisations are moving towards more open performance appraisal systems. Advances in technology and social media also call for some degree of openness.

How open should the performance management system be? I once saw a photograph of high performers (according to their evaluations) posing for a photograph with their chief executive officer after having been provided with a luncheon. This means that organisation allows its high performers to be visibly singled out and noted for emulation. There is, therefore, a level of openness in the outcomes of performance evaluation, at least as it refers to the best-performing employees. It would be de-motivating to have a similar openness with low performers without compromising their human dignity. In fact, managers are always encouraged to carry out public praise and private criticism. Openness also refers to the strategy goal-cascade process; the assignment of goals and objectives; clarity in the goal-setting process; and the feedback, developmental, and appraisal process. If these activities are viewed with secrecy or subjectivity, the basis of having the performance management system is undermined through the alternative interpretations and lack of standardization with which the entire process is viewed.

Performance Planning

Performance planning starts at the beginning of the performance period, when employees and their supervisors agree on the key objectives that the employee should focus on during the year. This discussion is held as a private discussion between the supervisor and the employee. The next step involves checking that all planned objectives of the department and of the company have been assigned to various individuals; otherwise they will not get done. This process of checking the completeness of the allocation of objectives to individuals is not a confidential or secret process as it involves discussions on who is best suited to carry out given tasks given the individual's seniority and experience and the task complexity. This may result in previously allocated tasks and corresponding objectives being shifted around. Because of the open nature of this practice, an employee will know who is assigned to certain tasks that were previously his own, and which tasks were previously assigned to others and are now allocated to him. I use the words *assign* and *allocate* fully aware that the goal-setting process or performance-contracting step is a collaborative one. This, however, does not negate the fact that the company objectives supersede any individual, group or parochial interests. The reasons for reallocation and reassignment, as well as the required performance standards, are also communicated to those who will carry them out.

I once went to a client and was about to start a meeting with the senior management. Before the meeting started, we were carrying out the usual pleasantries and finding out how all had been since the last meeting. In the course of the discussion, I found out that one of the senior officers had left the company, and I therefore asked if the officer had made any marked impact or shown improvement over the last few years. I knew that in posing this question I was venturing into performance assessment domain but did not state the question in such verbiage. One of the managers responded after thinking that he had not seen any progress or improvement apart from in minor administrative tasks. This brings us to the second aspect of *openness*. Individual performance is not in a vacuum. Managers and colleagues see and notice what kind of performance levels people demonstrate. They notice how people work, and they even notice the consequences of the different performance levels. A manager should therefore make it clear that employee performance is an open secret to which everyone in the organisation is privy either through direct observation, interaction or the reporting and management systems in place.

A large majority of the companies and organisations that I have worked with have scheduled weekly or biweekly management meetings in which the managers discuss the business performance of the company and its departments. These meetings are usually based on data and historical facts. One thing that at times lacks in such meetings is the discussion of the people aspect of the business in terms of past performance and pro jected results. The individuals and teams are at the centre of organisational performance. If the organisation has a spectacular week or month, it is because individuals and teams had a spectacular week or month. The spectacular nature of those weeks or months derives from how individuals aligned their performance goals with those of the organisation. The organisational performance is only an aggregate of individual performance. This particular aspect requires better communication among all stakeholders, so they can know the extent they need to consciously observe and record details of the performance of their colleagues. In a 360-degree performance appraisal system, feedback on employee performance is derived from multiple sources, including the customer, the supervisor, colleagues and subordinates. This appraisal method requires a number of prescriptions in order for it to be effective. These are:

1. What is the relative weight of the different feedback sources?

2. How does this relative weight contribute to the employee's performance evaluation or evaluation score?

3. How are the different providers of feedback developed in order to ensure that their feedback is complete, impartial, aligned and usable?

The feedback provided by customers, colleagues and subordinates may not fully capture the essence of an incumbent's role as would that of the supervisor. The supervisor's feedback for its part would lack some of the behavioural indicators which are best observed by people in the midst of everyday work activities. Peer feedback or feedback from colleagues also contains a unique flavour because these are the individuals with whom the incumbent sits at the same table either in management meetings, supervisory events or even on the shop floor carrying out designated tasks. A 360-degree feedback or appraisal process is therefore an open appraisal method.

For individuals to be able to provide meaningful feedback, they need to understand what the characteristics of that feedback should be, and they need to relate their feedback to the key objectives that the organisation seeks to achieve through the collaboration of the various individuals and groups. A subordinate, for example, should be able to provide feedback on both his direct supervisor's workplace competencies and how that supervisor fosters a productive environment in which the objectives of the organisation can be achieved. If one's subordinate is to be given effective feedback the organisation should be open about what the subordinate should observe and how that observation relates to a performance rating, score or qualitative feedback comment. The subordinate also needs to know that he must under no circumstances use the opportunity for retaliatory purposes or to achieve personal aims. Organisations will obtain feedback from multiple subordinates in order to eliminate the effect of bias, but the fact that feedback is skewed is not something to ignore—because in the outliers could lie the real essence of isolated incidences or behaviours which need to be corrected or which other pockets of employees are too scared to speak about. Opening of feedback to multiple sources increases its objectivity, provided that those providing the feedback are adequately schooled on how to do it effectively.

Performance Feedback

Jane was a customer service assistant in a medium-sized bank. She, however, rarely carried out the work she was hired to do. She was absent from her desk most of the time, and people assumed she had gone out to visit customers. One day her supervisor called her to his office, and it took her quite an amount of time to get there. When she arrived, he asked her for a status update of the customer issues she was facing. She responded only that customers were difficult and required a lot of attention. Peter, her supervisor, told her that her absence from her place of work showed a disconnect between what she did and what her customers expected, and it also raised questions about the activities she spent her time on. Jane's behaviour did not improve; however, she tried to conceal her whereabouts by leaving papers and files on her desk and a different jacket on the back of her chair. Peter noted these changes and on close follow-up noted that nothing had positively changed in Jane's work practices. Peter then told her that her inability to communicate her whereabouts was negatively affecting customer satisfaction and overloading the rest of the team members with her tasks. By demonstrating the impact Jane's omissions were having on the department, Peter gave her effective feedback. Performance feedback is the ongoing process between an employee and a manager, during which information is exchanged concerning the performance expected and the performance exhibited. Constructive feedback can praise good performance or correct poor performance and should always be tied to the performance standards.

From a performance improvement perspective, people require and deserve information on how well they are doing. Therefore, performance management makes use of tools, techniques, and systems that the manager or supervisor can use to support giving people feedback. The information should be timely, relevant and useful. It should be specific enough for people to act on, as feedback plays an important role in helping people deliver the expected results.

Feedback relates to what has been observed and how it fosters or deters the achievement of departmental or organisational goals. It should not be left to the end of the year or negative information only. The process of collecting and giving feedback should be planned for so that both the manager and the employee are clear on when formal feedback is going to be provided and from which sources that feedback is going to be obtained.

In most organisations, the primary person evaluating employee performance and thus providing feedback is the immediate supervisor. But more and more organisations are involving other people in the evaluation process. In many jobs, the immediate supervisor may not have access to all of the relevant information about employee performance. Imagine, for example, a police officer who spends most of his time patrolling the neighborhoods with his partner or a salesperson who spends most of her time meeting with customers. The supervisor may have information about the bottom line including the number of arrests made or the amount and value of sales. The supervisor, however, would have no information about the process contributing to those outcomes. In these cases, coworkers and customers may be able to fill in the gaps. At some organisations, employees are encouraged to identify a couple of coworkers with whom they work closely; at review time, the manager asks these "accountability partners" to evaluate the employee's contributions. Other organisations gather feedback from internal or external customers to evaluate sales and services employees. Some organisations are also involving employees' subordinates in the performance evaluation process. Subordinates can provide useful feedback to the manager about his or her management skills. These upward appraisals are especially beneficial for higher-level executives, who are often excluded from traditional top-down appraisal systems. Performance appraisal systems that involve multiple raters in the evaluation process are called *360-degree systems*. By inviting supervisors, subordinates, peers and customers to participate in the evaluation process, the employee can receive performance feedback from every possible vantage point—from above, below and on all sides.

The 360-degree feedback system works as an appraisal system for managers who are evaluated by a "circle" of people who frequently interact with the manager. It has been proven quite difficult to implement 360-degree feedback in large organisations due to the demanding nature of obtaining feedback from a cross section of stakeholders. Using 360-degree feedback, evaluations are limited to job behaviours directly observed and are primarily used as feedback devices. One of the criticisms of this system is that it lacks accountability due to the fact that most times feedback is provided in an anonymous manner, thus making it hard at times for the manager to situate the comments without resulting in witch-hunting and blame games.

Three-hundred-sixty-degree feedback can involve a handful of raters, or many. Three-hundred-sixty-degree feedback can be very useful in the performance appraisal process, especially in its ability to provide the employee with developmental feedback. People may be completely unaware of their strengths and weaknesses in interpersonal relationships unless the people they work with provide candid feedback about their behaviour. The key word here is *candid*—coworkers must feel comfortable in providing both positive and negative information to the employee. For that reason, the 360 feedback collected by an organisation is usually aggregated and summarised before being presented to the employee. This preserves the confidentiality of the individual raters and gives the employee a "big picture" view rather than pages and pages of detail.

Case Study 5: Genie Catalyst Drives for Openness

Genie Catalyst is a service company that had existed for a long time and had initiated a process of revamping its performance management processes. As it went through the redefinition of its performance management process it also decided to build on the provision of feedback as a way of increasing openness and objectivity. As part of this process, it introduced anonymous 360-degree feedback for all its managers. Employees would receive a form with a number of questions and respond based on how their manager had exhibited the detailed behaviours. The feedback would be compiled and delivered to the manager in a one-on-one session by their unit director. The director then provided the feedback verbatim as it had been stated by each individual manager's subordinates. The company also reinforced the provided feedback with observation. Observation was employed to assess how well individuals were living the values and complying to overt standards. A couple of times female employees were called to their manager's office or to the HR office to hear why their attire did not conform to the dress code. Some of the ladies argued that since they were not having meetings with customers, they did not feel that their attire was wrong. Others noted that there were male employees who did not don ties but were never called upon to explain why.

Does this feedback help an employee to achieve the organisational goals? Does the inconsistent application of feedback processes support its institutionalization in an organisation?

The organisation was using open feedback to handle behavioural issues outside the purview of the supervisor but was not open when it came to observable traits that were visible for all to see. When openness is practiced it should be comprehensive and not seem to be targeted at limited sections of the employee population.

Using Performance Feedback

Performance feedback is useless unless the performance expectations have been defined as described in Chapter 4, "The Format of Performance Expectations." The feedback will be given on the basis of the results that have been seen through the work of the employee. In the case of quantitative goals, the manager is able to discuss with the employee how well he has done and explore reasons, both positive and negative, for the performance. On the basis of performance feedback, managers can adjust the goals in order to better reflect the employee's capability and the external environment. Managers should always be involved in the work of their team members so that they can fully understand the conditions in which the team works, and so that they can see the team members in action. It becomes important for a team member to know that the feedback he is receiving is not from a third party but is based on his manager's own observation. The feedback from the team member is as important as the feedback the manager provides. In fact, it is how the manager is able to fully understand the situation and make the right adjustment based on evidence rather than just guessing what might solve a problem.

Modern-day athletes and sportsmen use a variety of tools to enhance their performance. They use coaches, video recordings and other tools to get the right feedback to improve their performance. In the corporate world, customer service engagements use voice recordings between customers and suppliers of services in order to enhance service quality as well as to have a basis for performance improvements and feedback. The goal of performance feedback is to improve skills and generate more revenue for the organisation. When a team member gets feedback on how his word choices may negatively affect customers, the feedback should give him new ideas on how to convey the same message; now he is put in a position to make more customers happy.

Ironically, the change will probably reduce the consistent conflict he experiences with customers, thus improving his overall job satisfaction. How the feedback is given is therefore as important as giving it. The athlete does not complain when his coach tells him that he needs to change a certain aspect of his movements in order to achieve more success or win more events. The athlete, in fact, spares no effort to get the movements right, as the tracker fixed on his sports equipment might suggest the need for change. In contrast, the nonathlete tends to react negatively to feedback. When managers are able to document feedback accurately, this negative reception of feedback will definitely decrease. It is thus said that feedback is the breakfast of champions.

The human attitude to reject negative or developmental feedback emanates from a lack of self-awareness and sometimes from a lack of evidence to back up the feedback. It is hard to change something if one is unaware of what one is doing wrong. This is most true with behavioural adjustments but holds true for detail-oriented tasks and processes as well. Someone who is taking too long to complete a client intake form might not realise a very simple trick on his keyboard allows him to toggle from screen to screen, thus saving him minutes per intake form. The old saying "You don't know what you don't know" is resolved with performance feedback. People learn what gaps they have and are able to adjust, saving time, money and often frustration. Observation and familiarity with the job task is key for one to be able to deliver such impactful feedback.

There are many forms that feedback can take. There is the immediate job-content-related feedback that managers provide to their staff, and then there is the periodic performance feedback provided on an annual or semi-annual basis.

Performance feedback can cover any area of business operations. Managers should periodically provide feedback to their staff on the following areas:

- **Quality and quantity of work:** This is a fundamental responsibility that employees need to get right. If someone's job is to prepare financial accounts and the work is done with errors, this is a problem for the company and its stakeholders. If this is a regular problem, it needs to be addressed. Feedback would include rating the quality of work, perhaps on a scale of one to five and noting the good and the bad to include regular mistakes. In many cases the quality of work might be acceptable but the quantity is unacceptable; for example, an auditor might be producing good audit reports but is always two months late. Or in the sales world, a salesman is able to sell telephone handsets but not enough to hit the agreed targets assigned to him.

- **Work habits:** This is an area of performance feedback that doesn't always seem like it affects performance, but it does. Being on time, dependable and organised seem like arbitrary performance items. But if someone is not at work, they are unable to help customers, and then other employees get burdened with additional duties. A person who is not organised might spend an extra ten minutes looking for a report, and thus arrive late to a meeting, creating a negative tone from the start. There are those who argue that not keeping time is not a cause of panic when done by executives. I counter this argument by saying that the executives must show the way through their actions and reinforce aligned behaviours through recognition mechanisms.

- **Service habits:** These habits affect an outsider's view of your company's competence and their desire to work with you. If an employee is not returning phone calls, is rude or transfers responsibility to others, customers will have a negative experience, and it will also strain employee relationships. Feedback in this area would include creating systems to make time for service issues and training on communication skills.

- **Team skills:** Some people work better in groups than others. There are those who get huge levels of anxiety leaving the safety of their cubicles. Helping your team understand how to work with each other, help each other and support each other is critical to preventing miscommunication or work slowdowns. If someone with a strong personality is constantly criticizing the person who is very introverted, your feedback may revolve around communication skills and inclusion ideas. Bringing the two parties together in a less anxiety-producing environment can improve productivity for both. Such an initiative, however, requires an understanding of human personality as it relates to your individual team members.

The Performance Feedback Action Plan

When a manager sees a problematic area in any part of the organisation, he must start the conversation and get employee input to develop a performance feedback action plan. This feedback action plan details how the employee will address the concerns provided through feedback. It could also require the employee to state what support he would like to receive in order to address performance gaps.

Feedback improves individual and organisational performance; in fact, it has often been said that feedback is the breakfast of champions. For feedback to result in improvements in individual performance, the feedback must be given in a suitable manner. When feedback is overly critical, employees might decide to ignore what they are being told because it makes them focus on the negative. Feedback given in an overly friendly way might not result in change either because the employee might not perceive it as important.

Due to the importance of feedback, organisations create processes for giving performance feedback. Some organisations give feedback on an interim basis by the performance manager and final feedback once an internal body has moderated or calibrated the performance reviews. This is what is referred to as *formal* or *institutional feedback*. It is the kind of feedback that organisations mandate managers to provide to their employees. This kind of feedback collates the behaviours and performance results of employees over half a year or a full year. Notwithstanding the importance of formalized feedback, managers must also create time to provide employees with informal, regular and timely feedback. The performance management philosophy has a great impact on the quality, timeliness and frequency of feedback and should thus be reviewed to ensure that the desired results are not delayed due to the adoption of the wrong focus.

You may use a form such as the one shown here to document the feedback provided and the agreed employee actions including a timeline within which to address the shortfalls.

Table 5: Feedback Action Plan Template

Employee name: *Job title:* *Department:*	*Manager name:* *Date of feedback:* *Date of completion:*

FEEDBACK PROVIDED

1) _____

2) _____

3) _____

EMPLOYEE ACTIONS TO ADDRESS FEEDBACK

Actions	Due dates
1) _____	1) _____
2) _____	2) _____
3) _____	3) _____

Employee signature	*Manager signature*

Regular feedback when practiced well helps individuals perform better. The following conditions should be adhered to when giving feedback in order to make it effective:

1. **Standards:** Determine what is normal for the performance item in question. Set expectations so that employees know the standards of performance. Sales numbers are easy to define metrics, but other performance items are not as easily defined. Take the time to look at the activities involved with any performance item and establish realistic parameters. This could be accomplished by looking at other employees and getting their input or by doing the task yourself to determine what is reasonable.

2. **Constructive language:** Use constructive language when providing performance feedback. This goes back to the point that people don't like to be criticised and will often block out any information coming with that criticism. An easy way to be constructive is to include the well-executed activities while also addressing the poorly executed ones. One organisation I have worked with used a system that began by telling the employee three things they did well and three things they could improve in. This creates a balance between positive and developmental feedback.

3. **Consistency:** Be consistent with all employees. If employees feel they are being singled out, it feels like a personal attack. At the same time, if you provide performance feedback only when things are going poorly in the organisation, you are not fulfilling the purpose of on-going conversations, and you are missing opportunities to fix things before the problem becomes exaggerated. Hold regular performance feedback sessions with all employees, and be open to new ideas and thoughts being brought up in good times and bad.

Case Study 6: Credible Bank's Performance Calibration Process

Credible Bank is the largest bank in its geographical territory. It has a strong branch network with presence all over the country and employs over two thousand employees. The bank has an annual turnover of over $120 million and a strong retail business. The bank felt that in order to improve fairness in its performance management practices, it would review its policy. The policy requires that managers carry our interim reviews for their staff at the end of the year. The ratings for each employee are submitted to senior management in what is referred to as a calibration committee. The committee goes through the performance ratings and comments in order to rationalise the results as well as ensure fairness and alignment to the organisational performance. The committee uses data to verify whether the performance standards used throughout the expanse of the bank have been consistently and fairly applied. They ensure that there is no leniency or severity in the appraisal process and that all possible errors and omissions have been accounted for. The outcome of this is that some ratings remain the same, others are increased and still others get reduced.

The revised ratings from the calibration committee are based on careful analysis of data, trends, and individual and team performance and become the final ratings for the period. Managers are then required to communicate the outcomes to their staff.

Employees whose ratings get reduced are very displeased with this process. They argue that the senior managers do not have firsthand information about their performance in order to downgrade their ratings. They also feel their managers do not adequately represent them in the performance discussions.

Is there something wrong with how this moderation process is carried out? Is it simply a communication issue?

Mistakes in Giving Feedback

Here are some of the mistakes managers and supervisors make that add to the pain of giving feedback:

- They avoid giving feedback on a regular and consistent basis but wait until the activity is painful for everyone.

- They assume people know how they are doing and think silence is sufficient feedback.

- They overlook the numerous daily or weekly opportunities to say they like what they see or to ask questions when they are in doubt.

- They do not take the time to establish goals, identify measures, and seek opportunities for feedback with their people.

- They confuse conclusions with feedback.

- They forget that giving feedback is a major part of their job.

Feedback is information about the past. It is the information people expect after they have done something to know whether what they did was adequate. It tells them whether they should proceed in the same manner. Feedback is information about how one performed in comparison with what was expected. However, feedback is effective only when it informs, when it guides people to behave in ways that lead to the desired results. Unfortunately, statements like "You're late," "You're over budget," "You lost the account," "You can't get along with people" or "You're not a team player" are really conclusions and do not provide sufficient information for people to know what to do differently. They do not communicate what was observed or what was used as the basis for comparison. The key is being specific about the behaviours, criteria or results that led to your conclusion and what it is you want someone to continue doing, change or stop doing.

Coaching is information about the future and is what people deserve before they set out to do something so they are more likely to do what is right and do it in the best way. Coaching is not criticism about what people did wrong or failed to do in the past, but is about what they should do as they undertake an assignment.

However, too often feedback is associated with giving people bad news and coaching is associated with trying to correct someone's behaviour instead of encouraging new behaviours. Because feedback and coaching are so closely associated with something being wrong, managers and supervisors tend to avoid them. Instead, they rely on silence to communicate that all is well and hope people will figure out what is wrong or how to do what is right. Being asked to give feedback or to coach often means being the bearer of bad news.

You can use tools to help you communicate your expectations, then compare the behaviours you observed and results achieved to what was expected. Ideally, you can leverage the tools that were used in doing the work. For example, the tools people use to execute plans, manage projects, develop products, or follow a process can also be used to monitor their own performance. The tools include project plans, action plans, budgets, statistical process reports and meeting management protocols. However, for these tools to provide feedback, the people using them have to track and compare what was done and how it was done with what was planned. Unfortunately, plans and budgets are created at the beginning, but actual time and costs are rarely captured and compared to the original estimates. If they are tracked, it is done at the end of the project when it is too late to take corrective action to improve the results. How many resources were used (people, time, materials and money) compared to what was estimated is valuable information, but not if it comes too late to act on.

Timely feedback lets the people responsible for estimating know whether they should improve the methods they use to scope out work. Knowing whether the estimates were high or low compared to what actually occurred is how you improve. Knowing the difference between planned and actual allows you to identify the circumstances and factors that inflated either the estimates or the end results. This information is feedback if people use it to guide them in estimating jobs in the future. It is information you can use to judge the adequacy of someone's performance so you will know whether you should use him or her in the same capacity in the future.

Budgets can also provide useful feedback; however, once they are built, people rarely see how expenses compare to what was planned. A person may approve an expense item, but he or she may not always see the cumulative effect on the overall budget. As a manager or supervisor, you can make sure people see running totals. You can also meet to discuss the work that has to be done, ask for different ways to accomplish it and guide your people to make wiser decisions about how to best use budgeted funds.

Guidelines have been developed to help people run feedback sessions more efficiently and effectively, but unfortunately these guidelines are not always used. However, having such guidelines can be very helpful when giving people feedback about why meetings went well or not. To some a meeting is an activity that affects work that is being carried out, while to others meetings are the way work gets done. Simple guidelines like the following can be used:

- Set objectives for meetings—define the outputs before you begin

- Decide on your outcomes—be clear on what you want the participants to do after and as a result of the meeting

- Start and end on time

- Stick to an agenda

- Document points or issues more appropriate for another meeting and commit to following up by a specific date

- Ask people to focus their attention on the subject under discussion instead of having sidebar conversations

- Choose how the group will decide, whether to formally vote on issues or use consensus

- Ask members who are quiet during discussions what they think and whether they want to add something to the discussion to assure that everyone is engaged and all opinions are counted

Structured in this way, meetings can be used as a method of collecting feedback as well as be organised to provide individual and group feedback.

Reasons for Performance Appraisals

Performance appraisals are one of the more disliked aspects of being a manager. Employees, too, find the process unrewarding. A reason they are ineffective is that people are unable to see the connection between what is talked about, what was expected, what was measured and what they did.

Yet performance appraisal systems are supposedly put in place to help you judge individual and team performance, help employees understand what is expected of them and help the organisation make compensation decisions.

Performance appraisals are imposed by an organisation for many reasons, among them:

- To assure that managers set and communicate annual goals with their people.

- To align people's attention and work goals with the needs of the organisation.

- To measure how well people accomplished the goals.

- To assure that people receive, at a minimum, quarterly feedback on how well they are doing. Annual performance appraisals are not a substitute for feedback in terms of supporting performance, as the information people receive is too infrequent and removed from what they do over the course of a year. The performance appraisal system may even track factors that are different from what you consider to be important. The annual review is not the event for people to hear for the first time that they are on track, need to improve their performance or need to correct their performance.

For performance appraisals to be effective:

- Managers and supervisors must be held accountable for conducting the formal reviews, setting targets, polling constituents, giving feedback and making adjustments as appropriate.

- People must believe the criteria used to evaluate them is fair and within their control.

- More than one set of measures should be set for judging performance.

- Managers should have the skills to communicate expectations, give feedback and recognise the difference between adequate and deficient performance.

- Annual performance appraisals are done at the individual and team levels. Department and division performance are usually evaluated based on meeting long-term strategic goals. Investors evaluate the organisation's performance by considering earnings, labour stability, growth potential, debt and other things.

Other requirements that employees must meet include:

- Complying with organisational policies

- Complying with safety regulations

- Being at work during work hours and when scheduled

- Cooperating with coworkers, customers and other business partners

- Complying with dress codes

- Documenting work performed, exceptions, customer issues and so on

Feedback should also be based on demonstrating the competencies that have been defined as being important for a given employee or group of employees. Organisations have rules about what measures to consider during the annual performance appraisal. Whether or not those measures are appropriate depend on the organisation's goals, the work unit's goals and the individual's developmental needs.

Some organisations dictate that every employee's performance measures should include at a minimum:

- The accomplishment of key objectives

- At least one developmental goal

Other organisations dictate measures that include some combination of the following:

- Team performance (goal accomplishment)

- Individual performance (meet quota or standard)

- Core competencies (leadership, communication and so on)

- Technical or job-specific competencies (Java programming, machine operation, financial analysis)

- Productivity goals (volume and quality of outputs)

- Customer satisfaction (ratings, retention, cost of service or sales)

- Product performance (reliability, shelf life)

- Financial performance (cash flow, cost avoidance, cost reduction, revenue)

These other goals make it difficult to connect the information exchanged during annual performance appraisals to what seems important on the job. A discussion on the sources of goals was made in Chapter 2, "The Employee in the Performance Management Equation." I suggest that you review that section in order to test your understanding of how you will provide feedback based on the identified sources of goals.

External Review

In many organisations, the feedback provided by a manager to his subordinates in an annual performance appraisal is not final. Managers are required to document the results of appraisals and then present these to a committee, which reviews all evaluations across the entire organisation. The purpose of this external review is to ensure that ratings and rating definitions have been applied consistently as well as to ensure that any form of bias has been eliminated from the process. This is done because the performance appraisal is also tied to other systems such as promotions, salary increments and bonuses. The committee that reviews such appraisals is variously referred to as a moderation committee, an appraisal round table or an appraisal review board. The committee makes adjustments to the ratings and then provides the adjusted ratings to managers who are then required to communicate them to their staff. The results are therefore calibrated or moderated in line with company performance and in line with established performance standards. *Performance calibration*, therefore, is a process in which managers (typically within a department or function) come together to discuss the performance of employees and achieve agreement on performance appraisal ratings. The practice of performance calibration refers to the steps taken to make sure that managers apply a consistent set of standards in making performance ratings. The process ensures:

- A fair and objective performance appraisal of past performance is made for each employee in relation to others in similar roles and/or job levels

- Managers apply similar standards to all employees

- Individual performance is aligned to the overall organisational performance

The fairness in performance appraisals is brought about through the institution of similar standards across departments. Managers in different departments are typically required to justify any exceptional and low per-formers while describing the behaviours or results that the individual con-tributed to or failed to contribute towards achieving. This allows the mod-eration team to ensure that individual performance has been appraised in a similar way throughout the organisation. Another important aspect of performance calibration is that of ensuring that individual and departmen-tal performance results are aligned to the organisation's results. If, for ex-ample, an organisation had set out to achieve a growth of 25 percent in its revenue, and a certain department involved in business development was not able to grow its revenue from the previous year but brings to the forum superior or exceptional performance appraisals of all or most of its staff, the calibration committee will not find alignment to organisational results because as a key contributor to the attainment of business goals the depart-ment cannot claim to have exceeded its expectations if they were unable to grow their revenue in line with the organisation's plans. The appraisals of the employees in this department would therefore have to be scaled down, even though the staff may have performed well in other areas, which could result in improved financial performance in subsequent periods. Perfor-mance calibration is not only about scaling down results of performance appraisals, but in some cases it results in scaling them up if a particular supervisor or manager has been too severe when appraising his staff.

After post-calibration changes have been made to performance ap-praisals, managers proceed to have their one-on-one performance review discussions with employees. At this point, managers should have a com-prehensive understanding of the organisational performance standards as well as how their team members have performed relative to others within and outside of the team. Managers should hone their communication skills so as to be able to pass their message to employees in a way that promotes productivity. Employees should not feel like victims or like they are on the receiving end of decisions which they don't particularly buy into. There have been cases in which, due to the manager's inability to communicate the results of performance calibration, employees have requested to appear in person to the calibration committee to explain why they deserve higher ratings. This should not happen if managers are able to communicate well and not distance themselves with decisions, since managers are also part of the organisation's leadership.

Performance calibration or moderation allows an organisation to make decisions related to the ratings as well as to rewards and recognition due to employees. A key advantage of having this system in the performance management process is that it ensures fairness and standardization across different departments and different managers. This is achieved by comparing the definitions of excellent performer, average performer and nonperformer in the different departments. It also removes the element of manager strictness or leniency from the process. Though it is practiced in many organisations it sometimes tends to be subjective and include an element of bias when the outcomes are not data driven.

Digital human resource and performance management systems have come up as a way to not only keep pace with the business demands but also to address some of the needs of the modern business. Digital human resource systems use digital technologies to collect, monitor and report on performance data. Digital HR is about identifying different ways in which technology can support managers and executives in those tasks that require data collection and analysis. In the case of performance calibration, the results of performance moderations are input into an online real-time system and communicated directly and immediately to the employee, thus eliminating any bias or need for a middleman. Organisations should also have a way of integrating documented portfolios of performance evidence from employees, especially if there are some borderline cases or if they can tell in advance that certain decisions are likely to result in disenchantment and loss of workplace harmony. An employee who understands what the performance requirements of his job are will maintain records and work samples of the work done to meet those performance requirements. This may take the form of client feedback, peer recognition, public acclaim in forums such as workshops, or even video clips of himself while engaging with customers or other stakeholders. The portfolio of performance evidence needs to be relevant only to the performance area under scrutiny.

The openness of a performance management system, therefore, must be determined by senior managers and executives and implemented by managers, supervisors and employees in a transparent manner. It is this planned and intentional openness that gives it credibility which in turn increases its usability and longevity.

CHAPTER 6

THE RIGOUR OF MEASURING AND MONITORING PERFORMANCE

"Whatever is worth doing at all is worth doing well."
—Lord Chesterfield

Rigour is closely linked to management and to the extent of sophistication that an organisation is ready to embrace. If what is being managed is simple, there is no need for a complex system; however, when the variables and behaviours being tracked increase, one begins to ask questions on how to improve the performance management system in order to address the internal and external complexities that it seeks to manage. The openness dimension is about looking at the elements of performance and determining who should receive the outputs of performance discussions including moderations. The rigour dimension ensures that no aspect of performance is excluded in rendering a full, transparent and objective view of not only the performance of the employee, but also of teams, departments and the organisation as a whole.

A rigorous performance management system is one that is exhaustive in its use of performance management tools at all stages right from planning, review, performance improvement, moderation and rewarding performance. It is about ensuring that no step is skipped for the sake of convenience and that all relevant stakeholders or actors are included as and when required. Rigour is in the interest of the organisation as it ensures that the pursuit of organisational goals and objectives is sanctified through putting in place accurate and complete measurement and tracking systems. Rigour is also in the interest of employees as it reduces complaints and feelings of unfairness since every outcome is traceable through the intermediary outputs and linked to the planned goals and objectives as well as to all forms of feedback and improvement actions that were discussed between the performance periods.

The format of performance management tools is key to this dimension and the degree of formality or informality within them. A good performance management system includes elements of both formality and informality in the application of tools. A performance dialogue, for example, is an informal method of addressing performance challenges in the course of the performance period. The manager may or may not take notes of this discussion, but the effect of it in improving employee performance depending on how well it is carried out is very important.

One of the biggest assumptions managers make when managing employees is that employees know what is expected of them because they signed a contract and because they have a job description. As a manager you would be fortunate to have such employees, and you would be even more fortunate to have all your employees, all the time, fulfill that premise. This chapter helps managers to work in a more systematic manner and avoid assumptions or generalisations. It helps them to apply the rigour that is required to enhance objectivity and fairness. It is also a fact that a job description needs to be interpreted or applied within an organisational context as defined by the strategy. A salesperson might know how to interact with customers and sell a company's products, but when the same salesperson moves to a different organisation he needs to understand the sales metrics that will be used, the sales process, the link between sales and the organisation's objectives, as well as the tools that the new organisation uses. This means that even though he or she is an accomplished salesperson, the new organisation has its own measurement and monitoring system to which he will need to adapt. The employee needs to apply rigour in making sure that he understands all elements of the organisation's landscape that have a bearing on his job. He must not wait to be told but should proactively seek to understand. An example of how an employee can do this was demonstrated in Chapter 1's introduction of the PERFORMANCE framework.

In order for the organisation to be successful, you must monitor the work that your employees do on an ongoing basis. This implies that you need to keep reminding employees what they must do to achieve specific goals. Monitoring employees helps managers keep abreast of employees' progress and assists in finding solutions that may be hindering organisational growth. In the case of high performers, monitoring in this way keeps them focused on the goals they must accomplish as well as on higher-level goals that they can pursue to grow their careers. Monitoring methods range from those that require management intervention to employee self-monitoring and the use of automated methods and checklists. The figure below illustrates that the aim of performance monitoring is to provide coaching to address identified gaps or lapses.

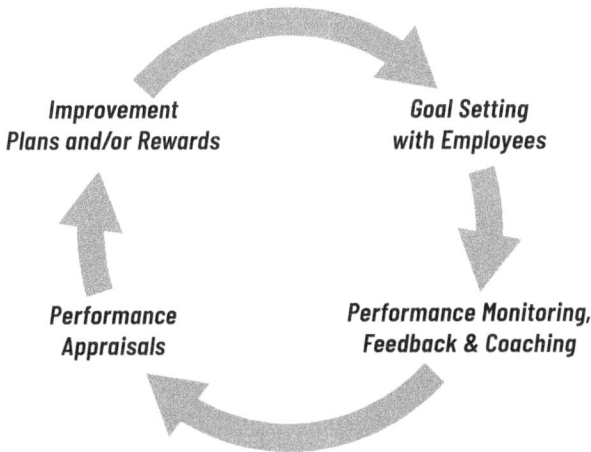

Improvement
Plans and/or Rewards

Goal Setting
with Employees

Performance
Appraisals

Performance Monitoring,
Feedback & Coaching

Performance Monitoring

There are a number of ways or techniques that can be used to monitor the performance of employees. The first part of this section discusses those techniques that are a result of direct manager intervention.

Establish Clear Expectations

Setting clear expectations is the starting point for any measurement or monitoring activity. In order to help your employees perform effectively, it's critical to have clear job descriptions for each role. These help your employees understand what they are responsible for and what their colleagues are responsible for. Managers should make sure that they draft a detailed job description for each employee that includes a list of duties they need to complete as part of their role. A description of what responsibilities they have should also be provided.

Once the job description has been developed, it should be shared with each employee. Have them review it and sign off on it, confirming their understanding of their role and accepting their duties. This is an effective way to establish a baseline for performance metrics, as the job description clearly outlines what needs to be done by each individual.

In addition to job descriptions, department managers or senior employees should create daily or weekly task lists for each area of the business. This helps employees understand what needs to be done by a particular time. For example, have a list of duties that customer service needs to complete each week and a list that the warehouse needs to complete each week. If necessary, format the list with a space for check marks, so employees can note when each task is done. I have seen many manufacturing companies using task lists in their factories. The task lists are constantly updated in order to keep the team informed of ongoing tasks and tasks that are about to start. In the not-for-profit sector organisations also use checklists to monitor the work being carried out by field staff.

In addition to ensuring each employee thoroughly understands their high-level job description, make sure they have a full comprehension of what's expected of them within each specific project, including detailed deadlines. This method usually works well within the manufacturing setup where employees are housed in a similar workspace. They are able to see scorecards in different sections of the factory and their performance in key aspects such as production and safety. In a knowledge-based workspace the scorecards can also be developed and shared electronically. Task dependency also means that one team might be responsible for an output which is the input to another department; so sharing expectations between such departments is important, and a monitoring plan should be agreed so that one department's delays do not negatively affect the work of another department. There are some instances when the required output from one department that forms the input to the next department can be partially shared as it gets completed; this way the receiving department is not kept waiting or guessing about the form the final output will take.

Another way to make sure your employees know exactly what they're supposed to be doing is to have them create goals for themselves, complete with a timeline for when each specific goal will be met. In order to achieve the best results that are the most easily trackable, have them utilise the SMART goal-setting method (specific, measurable, achievable, relevant and time bound), and keep track of their goals with task management software. There are many task management software applications in the market, and a good number of them are free of charge. Some existing office applications also have inbuilt task lists or schedule templates that an employee can use or share within a team. You should encourage your employees to be organised by keeping track of their tasks and prioritizing them based on strategic impact, impact to the department or team, impact to customers and impact to one's personal development and goals. This kind of prioritizing is useful, especially when a task takes longer than planned or when some unexpected changes occur. An employee can quickly adjust his task list based on the priority assigned or even defer the current task in order to complete an urgent task that might be slipping.

Set Performance Goals

In setting performance goals, you need to develop strategies to monitor team performance, including setting expectations and key performance indicators. Key performance indicators are discussed in the next chapter. During the annual performance evaluation meeting, managers set goals for the next year for each employee. This may include sales targets, campaign metrics or customer service feedback. Managers should also provide quantitative benchmarks that each employee needs to meet. These quantitative benchmarks are a way of introducing measures to set targets so that it is easy to track and follow up on progress. Even in situations that require customer engagement, the number and type of engagement sessions or activities should be determined up front, as should the expected results of the engagement.

Periodically Engage with Staff

Managers should have fortnightly or monthly check-in meetings with their employees. During these meetings with each employee or department, make sure you track the progress of each of the developed performance metrics. This way, you can ensure employees are on track towards meeting their goals. If they are far behind or far ahead, you may need to review performance or targets. You also need to check whether the performance metrics are geared towards obtaining the desired business results. A sample cheat sheet that you can use for this purpose is found in the appendix.

Measure Both Short-Term and Long-Term Performance

The most effective performance measurements encompass both short-term task completion and long-term performance. Long-term performance is a result of task completion and therefore gives a more accurate picture of true impact. You should find an online platform that lets you easily track short-term goals as well as long-term achievements, such as specific KPIs that can increase or improve over time. These online platforms come in different forms, and you should be careful to ensure that you do not overcomplicate or oversimplify the role of the online platform or tool. Measuring in the short term also provides you with an early warning of tasks that might be failing to meet expectations or even those that are surpassing expectations so that you can plan for them.

Online training software, for example, lets you easily measure each employee's impact, especially in relation to the training they've completed. Such platforms enhance the ability to compare certain KPIs with key training statistics to easily gauge the relationship between training and business performance.

Reverse Your Monitoring

One smart way of tracking employee performance is to go in reverse and start with the client or customer that the organisation serves. Figure out what motivated the client to use (and keep using) your product or service as this may be a key indicator of which employees were responsible for initiating (and keeping) the client. This information can also be supplemented with feedback from other employees themselves. Be cautious that personal or relational issues may result in skewed or subjective information, so always take employee feedback with prudence. If the employee is not in a client-facing role, going backwards would entail obtaining feedback from user departments on why they opt to obtain service from a particular individual in a given department. This monitoring also provides useful information for the performance of user and supplier departments, as the case of information technology departments proves. A number of employees in organisations get used to obtaining IT services from a specific individual in a department that has more than one staff member. Staff claim that this individual understands their needs best and is responsive to password resetting requests and other frequent troubleshooting instances. Reliance, however, on a single individual by a majority of the organisation's staff is unhealthy from an IT department point of view, as other staff resources remain idle and it puts a strain on the given individual. This monitoring would allow the IT department in such a case to carry out coaching to its other staff so that they can emulate the performance standards of the individual who gets the most requests for support.

Observe Employees While They Work

One of the most effective ways to monitor an employee's performance is with your own eyes. Watching an employee interact with a customer for a few minutes will tell you more about that employee's customer service performance than a batch of customer feedback surveys. That's why so many sales-oriented organisations encourage their managers to make customer visits with their salespeople. So the manager can actually watch the employee do his job. If you are having difficulties helping an employee succeed with a particular task, "shadow" that employee while he does the task. You'll find out exactly what he's doing and how he can do it better. If you cannot physically watch the employee work, you can record a video of the employee working with the employee's permission and use it as a basis of monitoring their work and supporting them in making gradual improvements. Managers can uncover a large amount of developmental needs that employees have by watching them work. I was surprised in using this method to discover that an experienced employee did not have the required spreadsheet skills to manipulate arrays of data. This gap made it seem that the employee was slow, while in reality the individual used a variety of manual methods to carry out analysis, which could be done on a spreadsheet with a few clicks.

Ask for an Account

In every one-on-one conversation with every employee, ask for an account of what that person has done since your last conversation: "What concrete actions did you take? Did you meet the clearly spelled-out expectations?" Then listen very carefully, make judgments and ask more probing questions. Asking for an account is the number one method for holding a person accountable for his actions. Then move on to discuss next steps. As long as you are consistently carrying out your one-on-one management conversations with every person on a regular basis, this element of monitoring performance will become routine. I had the fortune of working with a highly sales-oriented solar products company. The culture of the organisation was such that the field staff knew they had to deliver sales on a daily basis, as the responsible manager would ask for it. In attempting to improve this process, we introduced a number of tools which required the employee to give an account of what he had done and how he had used his time. This greatly increased sales and fostered accountability for results.

Help Employees Use Self-Monitoring Tools

You can also ask employees to help you keep track of their actions by using self-monitoring tools like project plans, checklists and activity logs. Employees can monitor whether they are meeting goals and deadlines laid out in a project plan, make notations within checklists and report to the manager at regular intervals. Activity logs are diaries that employees can keep, noting contemporaneously exactly what they do all day, including breaks and interruptions. Each time the employee moves on to a new activity, he is asked to note the time and the new activity he is turning to. Organisations such as law firms and management consultants use time sheets, which are completed on an hour-by-hour basis. Employees complete their time sheets online, and the manager is able to see what the employee has been doing and how he has used his time. In a bid to enforce transparency in spending, donors also require organisational recipients of donor funds to provide verified records of time spent carrying out the different intervention activities funded through a grant or other financing mechanism.

Implement Self-Monitoring Tools

You can promote self-monitoring tools which help employees to monitor their own performance as well. This helps them build the initiative to do well at work. It can also increase employee engagement and personal drive. Provide employees with project plans they can follow.

Coach them to create checklists and activity logs for their work so that they can set their own schedules while tracking their progress towards larger business goals. By giving them the tools to monitor their own performance, you help them build new skills such as time management, problem solving, conflict resolution and leadership.

The use of job aids, templates and reference guides is an important aspect of self-monitoring, as employees can cross-check activity sequence, sample deliverable and quality requirements against which to compare their current tasks, and make amendments as appropriate.

Employees should also be guided on compiling portfolios of performance evidence, which they should demonstrate to management from time to time. There are some information systems that allow for this to be done, but even if the systems lack this functionality, employees should have a way of showcasing what they have achieved, especially if it might not be immediately available or visible to the line manager. In the latter case, however, portfolios of evidence should be linked to the employee's performance contract and the associated key performance indicators of work performance.

Review Work in Progress on a Regular Basis

You should check your employees' work in progress carefully along the way. You should not wait for the finished product. If an employee is not responsible for producing a tangible end product, then watching that employee work is the same thing as reviewing work in progress. If she is responsible for an end product, spot-check it while she is working on it. For example, if the employee manages a database, spot-check the records. If the employee writes reports, look at drafts. If the employee makes phone calls, record them and listen to a random sample. If the employee makes widgets, check some half-done widgets and see how they look. You cannot actually keep track of everything every employee does, but you can check random samples on a regular basis. Cleaning and sanitary services that many hotels and offices require use this kind of review. The cleaning staff completes a form every time he carries out cleaning services. The supervisor uses the partially completed form to periodically carry out spot checks to ensure that the form filling was not an act of compliance but that the associated work was also carried out in the prescribed intervals. This method can be used in any kind of organisation, but gardeners and farmers have found it particularly useful as it also provides benchmarks on how much work can be done in a day by a particular type of individual. In the service industry the use of online group writing and commenting also allows the manager to see the progress being made on a shared deliverable such as a report and the relative input being provided by the team members working on it.

Obtain External Intelligence

This is not equivalent to going behind the backs of your employees but about gathering intelligence that is relevant to the work being carried out. You should ask customers, vendors, coworkers, and other managers about their interactions with specific employees so as to have an all-around view of the specific employee. You should ask questions only about the employee's work, never about the person. Don't ask for evaluations, but ask for descriptions. You should therefore not ask the customer or other party to rank the customer service provided by an individual relative to another individual. Don't ask for impressions, but ask for details. You should use open-ended questions that allow you to collect detailed information. And don't believe everything you hear; the unverified statements of third parties are simply hearsay. But the more you keep your ear to the ground, the more you know which sources can be trusted. So, ask around on a regular basis. The fact is that you are not the only one who interacts with your employees, and you should therefore seek a way of obtaining intelligence from external sources so that you can have ample information and evidence about trends and other observable patterns of performance in the workplace. Whatever you do in terms of obtaining this information, you should do it in a legal, ethical and professional manner, and the staff members should be aware that you are doing it.

Use Technology for Monitoring Staff Performance

Technology makes it possible to more easily monitor aspects of employees' jobs, although a policy on this subject should be considered before implementing it. In regard to privacy, the question of whether an employer should be allowed to monitor an employee's online activities exists. This may include work email, websites visited using company property and personal activity online. Another privacy concern can include monitoring of employee postings on external websites. When an employee posts something on social media, are they doing so as an employee of a certain organisation, and can the public including customers distinguish between posting as an individual and posting as a representative of an organisation? It is expected that companies will create more guidelines and policies to regulate this growing area in the future. Governments will also begin to legislate if concerns around this area continue to grow.

In order to make tracking progress and monitoring performance more efficient, implement technology solutions in your business. Tools that enable monitoring staff performance include those that allow management to see which tasks each employee has and how many have been completed. These tools also allow both employees and management to visualise the workflow for projects and see which areas are falling behind schedule. Team work-tracking software allows companies to track how much time employees are spending on each task in addition to viewing progress, while time and attendance software does that and also gives you a picture of the arrival and departure times to work.

There are many project management and performance tools available in the market; thus, you should select the one that provides the features you need for your organisation. Similar to the self-monitoring tools, managers can also implement groupware software that caters to online collaboration which makes the work of different team members visible to the rest.

Focus on Building Trust

One of the key ways of monitoring employee performance that is often ignored is building trust. It is a fact that no one wants to work with their manager constantly looking over their shoulder, wondering if they're up to the task at hand. That creates a hostile environment and can show employees that you don't trust them. Instead, empower your employees to do well at their jobs by providing them with the tools, training and expertise they need to excel. In the same vein, trust is broken when a manager goes against the set expectations and changes the rules of the game or goalposts midway between performance periods. If a manager consistently demonstrates this behaviour, employees are likely to resent him and lose trust in his ability to lead the team and bring out the best results. Trust is also affected by a manager's failure to recognise that employees are unique human beings, failure to take their views into consideration, failure to listen to them, or comparison of them to others with a view to making them feel inferior.

Monitoring performance in the workplace includes enabling your staff to have a hand in tracking their own performance with self-monitoring processes. This shows them that you believe in their abilities and want them to succeed. It shows that you trust them.

Provision of Feedback

In Chapter 5, "Openness of the Appraisal System," I described how an organisation should be purposeful in deciding upon the internal and external sources of performance feedback to be used. I also discussed the importance of feedback in helping both the employee and the organisation to improve and to learn from past mistakes and successes. Performance feedback is an ongoing process and is therefore key in promoting rigour within the entire process of monitoring, measuring and recognising results and outcomes.

A key element of monitoring employees is providing them with feedback. Feedback is critical because employees get to know how well they are performing in the different tasks assigned to them and how they are contributing to the success of the organisation. Employees who do not receive constant feedback do not know how well they are progressing and in what areas they need to improve. Feedback given on a timely basis creates an incentive for employees to excel in their performance.

The feedback provided should be specific and should be connected to specific incidents that both the manager and the employee can understand. Do not include information that has nothing to do with the employee's job performance. Further, ensure that you are qualified to provide the feedback. You must have an understanding of the employee and the employee's job requirements to be able to provide trustworthy feedback.

Feedback should not be left for once or twice a year. Feedback to employees should be provided as often as possible. As a manager you need to keep your employees motivated by letting them know how they are doing on a regular basis. An important note here is that you must provide immediate feedback on critical incidents so as to deal with problems as soon as they arise. A critical incident could be anything that derails the performance of the team, the unit or the department. It could also be a key element of the overall employee performance such as failure to collect accounts receivable within agreed timescales. When feedback is provided, the manager should end with helpful and supportive advice. Employees should not be left wondering what they should do next. For example, if your feedback informed an employee of his negative behaviour towards accounts receivable, end the feedback by providing him with positive steps he can take to improve his work attitude.

Whether it's in person or through the use of an employee training or coaching software, it's vital to have frequent check-ins with each of your team members. While the most ideal frequency is once a week, make sure to do this at least once a month. Ask them questions about the specific project they're working on, if they need additional resources and if they're having any problems or challenges, and have them provide a clear, detailed and explicit answer as to their progress on the specific project. Another way to complete this is to have each employee send an end-of-week update on everything they accomplished that week.

Use of Recognition

In order to keep monitoring accomplishments, it is important to use recognition. By consistently monitoring your employees, you learn who has satisfied and exceeded the organisation's expectations. You should make recognition an authentic day-to-day experience. There are many ways of recognising individual and group performance, including sending thank-you emails and offering verbal congratulations frequently to those who deserve it. Recognition is determined by the company culture, the employee preferences and the manager's degree of flexibility to exercise discretion. In spite of these, the little things matter a lot to employees—and if you cannot take your employee who has exceeded expectations for a luncheon or coffee, the least you can do is send a thank-you message or a congratulatory email because these do not cost you. Chapter 8, "Activities to Reward and Recognising Performance," provides more details on additional methods and techniques you can use.

Measure in a Way That Encourages Working Smarter, Not Longer

There are many shows on television that depict a manager arriving in the office in the morning and finding an employee who spent the night at the office working. In actual day-to-day work, the practice of working beyond the prescribed hours is still prevalent with both employees and managers who believe that this demonstrates commitment. Many companies are now starting to discourage this practice because it goes against not only work–life balance but also against the dignity of the individual and the family. A job by its nature is designed to be carried out during specified hours, even though there are emergencies that arise and that necessitate extra hours. Logging minutes and hours is becoming less common, and tracking task completion, accomplishments and deadlines is now the norm. The most important question to ask (and track) is this: Is the work getting done? In most organisations, where the work is done is no longer an issue. Many successful businesses are finding that it doesn't necessarily matter how, when or where tasks are being completed (from the office, from home, in a restaurant), but rather that the tasks are being completed and results are being produced. Using an online task platform with mobility and flexibility enables this sense of freedom.

Always Keep an Eye on the Bottom Line

Performance metrics may show that your team seems to be performing their tasks well and at lightning speed, but do your profit margins reflect this productivity? It's important to consistently compare your employees' productivity to your overall profits, because at the end of the day, this is what matters the most. Keeping an eye on high-level business performance can help you resist the urge to constantly micromanage and try to control every minor detail occurring on a daily basis.

One suggestion is to determine your team effectiveness ratio by measuring your gross profit not against the number of hours worked, but against the overall salary costs of your employees, because results and value are much more powerful metrics than the number of hours worked.

Relate Employee Performance to Management Style

In a similar way to obtaining intelligence from external sources, every manager should spend time with each employee. Part of this time spent should be used asking the employees how they view their own performance. While it is true that employees tend to rate themselves highly, this should not dissuade a manager from holding this conversation. You should also remember that performance management is a double-sided coin where your own attributes as a manager influence and affect employee performance and vice versa. You should not be so busy tracking your employees' performance that you don't give them a chance to evaluate you and your performance as a manager. This can be done through an in-person meeting or an online survey. You may even decide to make the survey anonymous to give each member of your team a chance to describe their perceptions of their roles, work environments, resources, training, your management style and other elements. This data can then be compared to their own performance statistics for an eye-opening and objective overview.

Case Study 7: Genie Catalyst's Financial Performance Reports

Genie Catalyst provides its managers with flash reports on a monthly basis that relate to the financial performance of the company. This report is used as a monitoring tool. The monthly report details variances of planned versus actual results in gross revenue, gross margin and gross profit. The reports at the time of writing do not provide a drill-down view of individual staff and teams, but they highlight the departments' performance on each of the key financial performance dimensions, thus allowing for corrective action on a monthly basis. The company also has a training calendar in which it equips managers with knowledge of key financial ratios and other financial-related information so that they can better interpret the business results and take action to address areas of concern.

The reports do not produce nonfinancial information; the company believes that its financial performance is the key determinant of its success. While financial reporting and monitoring is important to any business entity, there must be a consideration for other areas of the business, including customer management issues, innovation practices, general organisational health in terms of employee training, development, welfare and safety among others. Financial performance is only one element of a high-performing organisation.

Regular Performance Monitoring

Every organisation should continually monitor and evaluate its employees. There are seven areas in summary to quickly gauge performance and ensure your organisation is on the right track:

1. **Punctuality:** Employees who regularly arrive late for work or are frequently absent from the office are unlikely to be meeting their performance objectives. The underlying issue needs to be addressed here: Have they received adequate training? Do they get along with their coworkers and manager? Issues with punctuality mean an employee is not doing their job to their full potential, and a negative attitude may also be affecting their colleagues.

2. **Quality of work:** The timely completion of projects to the desired standard is a key indicator in measuring employee performance. Is the work being carried out average or outstanding? Are they committing maximum effort to projects? Is their attitude affecting their ability to meet your expectations? Do they understand their personal performance objectives? The answers to these questions will help you to understand the root causes of any problems.

3. **Observe personal habits:** Perpetual bad habits can detract from employee performance. This may include indulging in office gossip, taking unauthorised breaks, disruptive behaviour and the use of computers for personal reasons (such as social media or online shopping). In order to prevent these habits from being adopted by their coworkers, you must be clear on what is acceptable in your business and issue an appropriate behavioural code.

4. **Check their attitude:** A bad attitude will often manifest itself in insubordinate behaviour. Again, this is indicative of an individual who is unlikely to be meeting their performance objectives. Typically, these employees will not comply with company policies and are likely to display disrespect for your company and coworkers.

5. **Review personal presentation:** Most firms have a professional dress code appropriate to the job and company culture. Employees who disregard your expectations and present a disheveled or careless appearance reflect badly on your image. It's likely that their performance will be failing to meet your expectations too.

6. **Carry out a client survey:** The consequences of poor employee performance will ultimately manifest themselves in customer service. A client survey can quickly identify issues with individuals. A positive response means your employee's performance is meeting or exceeding expectations. What is the overall customer service experience of your key customers, agents, distributors, partners and so on?

7. **Carry out random checks:** Depending on the nature of your business, consider implementing random checks against quality standards. This may include reviewing telephone calls and checking records. While your employees may be aware of this policy, the random nature of the checks can motivate staff to put in a consistent performance.

Monitoring, measuring and evaluating employee performance should be carried out on an ongoing basis and encompass all areas of work ethic and individual achievements. It is important to note that poor performance or negative behaviours can also be symptomatic of an underlying problem with your organisation's culture, so have a plan in place to address any issues you discover.

Balancing Monitoring with Employee Well-Being

As you monitor and measure performance you should also ensure that you are not interested in performance at all costs. There are other elements that you should ensure are not upset or negatively affected. The health and safety of employees is one of these. You should not demand of your staff in such a way that their mental or physical health is compromised. You should also ensure that there is a work–life balance and that families are not broken as a result of seeking to achieve business results. You should ensure ethical business practices and that individuals and teams do not take shortcuts all in the pursuit of rewards and recognition. A performance culture achieves a balance between achieving business, personal and team results. If there is equilibrium between these three groups then the results are truly outstanding, even if the organisation has to forfeit a certain good in the interests of promoting the welfare of the families of its staff members. An ethical, family-friendly workplace is important not only for shareholder satisfaction but for employee satisfaction as well. Companies are seeing the value of implementing ethical codes within the business. Monitoring of compliance to the ethical codes and standards should be undertaken frequently. Some organisations downgrade an employee's performance ratings if they find that the performance has been achieved through any form of ethical misconduct.

CHAPTER 7

MANAGEMENT OF KEY PERFORMANCE INDICATORS

"Never give up on something that you can't go a day without thinking about."
—Winston Churchill

MANY PEOPLE WHEN ASKED THE question "What keeps you awake at night?" will tend to think of a myriad of negative things like stress, a relationship that's not working and financial troubles. The passionate manager and staff, however, are kept awake at night not by the negatives but by the excitement of the following day's work when they think of the prosperity and abundance they can create at work characterized by high value tasks and objectives.

Management's role within the performance management system is broad and at times complex. Some managers have been heard to ask how they can be expected to effectively play their role in driving performance while at the same time pursuing business results. This view of management is limited in the sense that the pursuit of business results is and should be part of performance management simply because managers achieve results through the efforts of others. Managers should carry out coaching activities geared at improving employee skills. *On-the-job coaching* is one way to facilitate employee skills development. On-the-job coaching refers to an approved person training an employee on the skills necessary to complete tasks. A manager or someone with experience shows the employee how to perform the actual job. *Mentoring* can also be used for skills transfer. Mentoring is a process by which an employee can be trained and developed by an experienced person. Normally, mentoring is used as a continuing method to train and develop an employee. Another method that management can use is *brown-bag lunch training* in which the training occurs during lunchtime, employees bring their food, and someone presents training information to them. The trainer could be HR or management or even another employee showing a new technical skill. Brown-bag lunches can also be an effective way to perform team training, as it brings people together in a more relaxed atmosphere. It is the role of managers to determine what training and non-training interventions they can apply or recommend for performance improvement.

KPIs, KRIs, PIs, Goals and Objectives

A common expression that one tends to hear during the performance cycle is that "we are in the process of setting KPIs for our staff" or that a given staff member did not achieve the set KPIs. Are these people really referring to KPIs, or is there a mix-up between KPIs, goals and objectives? What are KPIs and why do they matter in the performance management process? Aren't goals and objectives enough? Do we need another level of measurement to complicate an already complex process?

Key performance indicators (KPIs) represent a set of measures focusing on those aspects of organisational performance that are the most critical for the current and future success of the organisation. A goal, on the other hand, is the outcome that the individual or entity needs to achieve, while the objective quantifies the goal by adding measure. For example, a goal could be to grow the geographical footprint of the organisation, while an objective related to that goal could be to identify, select and launch operations in two regions in the current year.

A key performance indicator (KPI) is a metric that shows the fiscal health of your business and can represent whether you are successfully running your business, show long-range trends year over year, be the target you aim for everyday and inform you on where to focus training efforts. A KPI therefore provides information to tell you how well you are doing towards meeting your goals and objectives. KPIs are rarely new to an organisation. They have either not been recognised or were developed and left somewhere that the current management is not aware of.

Before delving deeper in the importance and use of KPIs, it important to understand other types of performance measures. There are three types of performance measures:

1. *Key result indicators* (KRIs), which tell you how you have done in a balanced scorecard perspective.

2. *Performance indicators* (PIs), which tell you what to do.

3. *Key performance indicators* (KPIs), which tell you what to do to increase performance dramatically.

Many performance measures used by organisations are thus a mix of KRIs, PIs and KPIs, which are sometimes not focused at the appropriate organisational level or completely jumbled. It is important to set appropriate performance measures not only for your individual employees but also for your departments and even for the organisation as a whole.

KRIs

As pointed out, KRIs tell you how you have fared in a given balanced scorecard perspective. They are measures that have often been mistaken for KPIs, including: customer satisfaction, net profit before tax, profitability of customers, employee satisfaction and return on capital employed. When you achieve a certain level of customer satisfaction, for example, this is a result that tells you how well you have done in the customer perspective of the balanced scorecard. The common characteristic of these measures is that they are the result of many actions. They give a clear picture of whether you are traveling in the right direction. They do not, however, tell you what need to do to improve these results. Thus, KRIs provide information that is ideal for the board (i.e., those not involved in day-to-day management).

KRIs typically cover a longer period of time than KPIs; they are reviewed on monthly/quarterly cycles, not on a daily/weekly basis as KPIs are. Separating KRIs from other measures has a profound impact on reporting, resulting in a separation of performance measures into those impacting governance and those impacting management. An organisation should have a governance report (ideally in a dashboard format), consisting of up to ten measures providing high-level KRIs for the board and a *balanced scorecard* (BSC) comprising up to twenty measures (a mix of KPIs and PIs) for management.

PIs

In between KRIs and the true KPIs are numerous performance indicators. These complement the KPIs and are shown with them on the scorecard for the organisation and the scorecard for each division, department and team. Performance indicators that lie beneath KRIs could include: profitability of the top 10 percent of customers, net profit on key product lines, percentage increase in sales with top 10 percent of customers, and number of employees participating in the suggestion scheme.

KPIs

A KPI must have seven characteristics for it to be a true KPI. The seven KPI characteristics are:

1. It is a nonfinancial measure and is thus not expressed in dollars, yen, pounds or euros.

2. It is measured frequently (e.g., daily or 24/7).

3. It is acted on by the CEO and the senior management team.

4. It is understood by all staff including the corrective action it requires.

5. It ties responsibility to the individual or team.

6. It has a significant impact; for example, it affects most of the core *critical success factors* (CSFs) and more than one balanced scorecard perspective.

It has a positive impact (e.g., it affects all other performance measures in a positive way).

When you put a dollar sign on a measure, you have already converted it into a result indicator (e.g., daily sales are a result of activities that have taken place to create the sales). The KPI lies deeper down. It may be the number of visits to contacts with the key customers who make up most of the profitable business.

KPIs should be monitored 24/7, daily, or perhaps weekly for some. A monthly, quarterly, or annual measure cannot be a KPI, as it cannot be key to your business if you are monitoring it well after the event it governs has happened and ended. KPIs are therefore current- or future-oriented measures as opposed to past measures (e.g., number of key customer visits planned in the next month or a list of key customers and the dates of their next visits. When you look at most organisational measures, they are very much past indicators measuring events of the last month or quarter.

All good KPIs make a difference; they have the CEO's constant attention, with daily calls to the relevant staff. A KPI should tell you what action needs to take place. British Airways had a "late plane" KPI which was communicated to everyone and made people note that there needed to be a focus on recovering the lost time. Cleaners, caterers, ground crew, flight attendants and liaison officers with traffic controllers would all work vigorously to save a minute here and a minute there, while maintaining or improving service standards.

A KPI is deep enough in the organisation that it can be tied to an individual. In other words, the CEO can call someone and ask "why." Some measures that organisations use as KPIs are a result of many activities under different managers and cannot be tied to an individual manager or employee. Return on capital employed is one such measure which cannot be tied to a manager as it is a result of many activities under different managers.

A good KPI will affect most of the core critical success factors (CSFs) and more than one balanced scorecard perspective. In other words, when the chief executive officer, management and staff focus on the KPI, the organisation scores goals in all directions. This is achieved through the interrelationship that exists between perspectives through the cascading process and also through the bottom-up congruence that is achieved when individuals at lower levels carry out activities which add up to achieve greater results higher up.

A good KPI has a flow-on effect. An improvement in a key measure within the CSF of customer satisfaction would have a positive impact on many other measures. Timely arrival and departure of planes gives rise to improved service by ground staff, as there is less "firefighting" to distract them from a quality and caring customer contact.

PAST MEASURES	CURRENT MEASURES	FUTURE MEASURES
Last week/two weeks/ month/quarter	*24/7 and daily*	*Next day/week/month/ quarter*
For example, number of late planes last week/last month	For example, planes over two hours late (updated continuously)	For example, number of initiatives to be commenced in the next month/two months to target areas that are causing late planes

10/80/10 Rule

The balanced scorecard, which is a tool that was developed by Dr Robert Kaplan and Dr David Norton, is a framework for measuring organisational performance using a balanced set of performance measures. These measures include financial, customer, internal business processes and learning and growth. Dr Kaplan and Dr Norton recommend not more than twenty KPIs in an organisation. Since they are key performance indicators, there should not be too many as that would reduce the impact and dilute organisational focus around too many performance areas. The *10/80/10 rule* is a good guide: there are about 10 KRIs, up to 80 PIs, and 10 KPIs in an organisation. Very seldom are more measures needed, and in many cases even fewer are used.

For many organisations 80 PIs will at first appear totally inadequate. Yet on investigation, you will find that separate teams are actually working with variations of the same indicator, so it is better to standardise them (e.g., a "number of training days in the last month" performance measure should be consistently applied with the same definition within different teams).

KEY RESULT INDICATOR (10)	Tells you how you have done in a given balanced scorecard perspective
PERFORMANCE INDICATOR (80)	Tells you what to do
KEY PERFORMANCE INDICATOR (10)	Tells you what to do to increase performance dramatically

When you have a business or departmental objective, you will realise that in order to achieve it there are a number of activities that need to take place in order to achieve the objective. If you offer accounting services, for example, you will want to increase revenue from accounting services. To do this you will need to make a number of calls to prospective clients or upsell a number of new services to existing customers.

The example below illustrates how you can create KPIs from objectives:

- **Objective:** Decrease employee turnover rate by 25 percent over the next quarter.
    - **KPI1**: Increase training hours per annum/per employee by 15 percent
    - **KPI2**: Increase number of employees who can articulate organisational values to 75 percent
    - **KPI3**: Reduce time to respond to an internal complaint to forty-eight hours

Importance of Timely Measurement

The use of measurement varies widely across the world. Many businesses use the balanced scorecard to create behavioural alignment in a balanced way. It is essential that measurement be timely. Today, a KPI provided to management that is over five days old might be useless. KPIs are prepared in real time, with weekly ones available by the next working day. The suggested reporting framework of performance indicators is that one or two KPIs should be updated daily or even twenty-four hours a day, seven days a week.

Most organisations will have five essential KPIs, which must be reported weekly at least (excluding the daily or 24/7 KPIs). Performance measures that focus on completion should be included. Projects that are running late and overdue reports should be reported to the senior management team each week. Such reporting will revolutionise project and task completion in your organisation.

The remaining performance measures should be reported on a monthly basis and include a team and business unit balanced scorecard.

The table below shows some of the key features of the different performance measures and examples of each:

PERFORMANCE MEASURE	AUDIENCE/ USERS	FREQUENCY OF PROVISION	EXAMPLES
Key result indicator	*Board or senior management*	*Monthly or quarterly*	• Customer satisfaction • Net profit before tax • Profitability of customers • Employee satisfaction • Return on capital employed
Key performance indicator	*Departments, managers or employees*	*Daily or weekly*	• Increase number of planned customer visits to two hundred • Reduce accounts receivable by 25 percent • Double sales volume over period • Increase upselling rate by 15 percent

			• Reduce absenteeism rate by 5 percent • Increase number of suggestions per employee to fifty • Increase net promoter score by 12 percent
Performance indicator	*Departments or employees*	*Daily or weekly*	• Performance of top 10 percent of customers • Net profit of key product lines • Percent increase in sales of top 10 percent of customers • Number of employees participating in scheme

STEPS FOR DEVELOPING EFFECTIVE KPIs
Start with Strategy

Before beginning the development of your KPIs it is important to consider your organisation's mission, vision and values (MVV) to guide the direction of your efforts. The MVV is your destination. Use your MVV as inspiration to create broad categories for your KPIs to fall into. This will make it easier to decide if a KPI is important or just another number to track. If it does not fall into one of the categories, then you can get rid of it.

We have seen the importance of starting with strategy when developing a performance management framework and ensuring that departmental goals and individuals are aligned to the organisation's strategy. Even when developing KPIs you should always start with strategy. The strategy gives you a good grounding on what your business is seeking to achieve. Because strategy is about selection and choice, you avoid the pitfall of ending up with a long list of possible indicators that you feel you could or should measure.

Your strategy therefore acts as a starting point for designing appropriate KPIs, provided that it is clear. Some companies create lengthy strategy documents that no one ever reads or understands. A great way around this is to create a simple one-page strategy. This will help you clearly define your objectives, and help you work out what you need to put in place to achieve them. You can also refer to your strategy map if your organisation uses the balanced scorecard system, as strategy maps are very useful strategy communication tools that help focus on the organisation's strategy. If you don't have a one-page strategy, request an interview with one of your executives and document the key strategic thrusts of your business or organisation. You can then proceed to create categories which your KPIs will fall into. Examples of these broad categories are:

- Growth

- Profitability

- Productivity

- Compliance

Define the Questions You Need Answers To

Linking your KPIs to your strategy will immediately sharpen your focus and make the relevant KPIs more obvious. Identifying the questions you need answers to will further narrow your focus, because questions give the indicators context. The key performance questions help you to figure out what data you will need to gather, and this will inform which KPIs you need to set.

For example, if you plan on executing a simple strategy to increase your income by focusing on the most profitable areas of your business, you could ask, "Where are we making profit, and which processes are most costly compared to the returns we receive?"

Once you are clear on the questions you need to answer, you can make sure that every indicator you subsequently choose or design is not only relevant to your strategy, but also provides the answers to very specific questions that will guide your strategy and inform your decision-making.

Identify Your Data Needs

Once you know what questions you're trying to answer, you must define your data needs to establish what KPIs, metrics or data you require to answer those questions. It is pointless to develop or identify a KPI that cannot be measured.

In this phase, you start by forgetting about reality for a moment and consider what information and knowledge you want to have in an ideal world. If you constrain yourself with the reality you currently face, you will limit your ability to improve business and operational performance. It is good to wear your hat that says everything can be measured!

Evaluate All Existing Data

Having worked out your ideal data in the previous step, perform a gap analysis by comparing what data you would ideally like to have with what you already have—that way you can easily see what's missing. Ask yourself what you need to change, tweak or implement to ensure the data collection is completely aligned with the strategy and will fully answer the questions you need answered. And then come up with the right indicators to deliver those objectives.

You need to remember that most companies are full of data. This data resides in a number of systems, both manual and automated, that reside within the organisation. Often KPIs are already being collected for all sorts of different reasons by different divisions and different managers. It makes sense, therefore, to determine whether what you need is already being gathered by someone somewhere in the business, or perhaps it is close to being collected and just a few tweaks to the process would deliver exactly what you need.

Find the Right Supporting Data

KPIs are incredibly powerful in the right hands, but we need to acknowledge that we also have access to vast quantities of supporting data that is every bit as insightful and useful as traditional KPIs. By finding the right supporting data related to industry information, demographic data, trend statistics or any other, you can assess and verify your findings. An example of such supporting data is an industry benchmark that relates the performance of the company against the KPI in relation to the industry, because on its own it might give the impression that the organisation is doing well when in fact it is not. For example, the industry gross profit margin in a given industry might be 20 percent, but the organisation with a 10 percent margin might believe it is doing well because it is able to achieve profitability through remuneration levels that are below the market average of its peers.

The datafication of our world, in which vast amounts of information are being created and stored every minute, means there is a great deal of supporting data that can potentially provide information that is relevant to your strategy. By finding the right supporting data, you can make much better sense of the world, much more quickly, which helps you make better, faster business decisions.

Determine the Right Measurement Methodology and Frequency

Knowing what you need is one thing—working out how to access and measure that information is another. Finding the right measurement methodology is critical. Therefore, once you know what information you need to collect, you need to find the right measurement methodology to get it. This is especially true if you have to develop new KPIs or tweak existing ones.

It's always preferable to align measurement frequency with how and when the data is used in the organisation, because all data has a "useful life." This means measurement frequency must be in line with reporting frequency. If it's not, the data may lose impact and/or relevance. For example, if you collect customer satisfaction data via a survey at the beginning of the year and report on the findings in the middle of the year, then the findings are already six months out of date.

Assign Ownership for Your KPIs

Effective KPIs require two types of ownership. The first is the ownership of the KPI in terms of its meaning and interpretation. Someone needs to be in charge of looking at the KPI, interpreting its meaning, monitoring how it's changing and deciding what that means for the business.

The other ownership refers to the data collection. Sometimes you can automate the process, but more often than not, data collection will require some human interaction. Perhaps certain employees are involved in transferring data from one database to another, or they have to collect it manually. Again, this ownership needs to be clearly set out and followed through.

Ensure KPIs Are Understood by People within Your Organisation

It's essential that everyone in your business is aware of what you're trying to achieve, and how you're measuring progress towards those achievements. This is especially important for those who are charged with ownership of the KPIs, but it's also important for people right across the business, at any level. KPIs should form part of the decision-making process for every employee, and everyone should be able to answer the question, "How will what I am doing today affect our KPIs?"

You, therefore, need to ensure everybody understands how the metrics you are gathering are linked to your strategic priorities. This will increase buy-in—how personally involved and enthusiastic your staff feel about your priorities—and ensure that constant review and improvement are at the heart of everything your employees do. If you simply tell everyone that they have to collect mountains of extra data from now on without explaining why, you are likely to end up with a very cynical and disengaged workforce!

Find the Best Way to Communicate Your KPIs

It's always wise to think about how best to communicate your KPIs so their insights are obvious, engaging and apparent to all. So many KPIs are reported in long reports full of numbers or tables, perhaps with a traffic light graphic to indicate urgency. This is not good enough. There is absolutely no point hiding important insights in excessively long reports that no one ever reads. Really effective visualisations clearly illustrate trends and variations in data and engage the reader. Try to find the right picture for your KPIs, and create an explanation of the insights so that the nuggets of wisdom extracted from the data are clear, unambiguous, accessible and most importantly actionable.

Make sure you align and customise your communication of KPIs to the specific audience. Tailor the message based on the stakeholders' expertise and interests, providing a high-level overview for executives and more detailed insights for operational teams. Ensure that you use visualisations and storytelling to convey complex data in an accessible way, fostering a unified understanding and commitment to organisational goals. You should communicate with empathy to employees so that they can clearly understand how their work contributes to the achievement of the communicated KPIs.

Review Your KPIs to Ensure They Help Improve Performance

If a KPI isn't useful in helping you or others in your business make better decisions, which in turn will improve your business's performance, then it's just noise. You therefore need to constantly review the metrics you are measuring to make sure they are genuinely useful and you aren't spending hours (or asking your staff to spend hours) measuring data simply to tick off boxes.

Used properly, considering vision and objectives, KPIs provide a vital tool for improving performance, making better business decisions and gaining a competitive advantage. An example of an organisational vision, objective and KPI include the following:

- **Organisational Vision:** To be known for our superior customer service and satisfaction

- **Organisational Objective:** To reduce the number of dissatisfied customers by 25 percent

- **Organisational KPI:** The number of customer complaints that remain unresolved at the end of a week

Once you have developed your KPIs you should document them in a format such as the one shown below. This allows you to communicate the KPI information to all stakeholders consistently, while also providing a means of training newcomers or new users of the information.

INFORMATION	DEFINITION	EXAMPLE/GUIDELINE
Performance Indicator	The performance indicator name or title, under the relevant performance theme (e.g. Revenue Growth)	N/A
Formula	The mathematical or logical formula; ultimately, the formula provides the data inputs to the performance indicator	Employee turnover = Number of employees exited/total number of employees
Target	The established target the organisation intends to achieve which aligns with strategic priorities and annual business plans	Monthly, quarterly, annual or multiyear targets
Purpose	The intent of the indicator; what it is trying to gauge	Helps user to understand its significance in organisational performance
Level of Use	The levels within the organisation that will use this indicator	e.g., department, branch
Status	Indicates if the indicator is currently tracked/measured or if it is new	Options include new or existing
Reporting Frequency	The frequency the indicator should be reported to management and should consider the timeliness, relevance, and relative importance of the performance information for decision-making	e.g., weekly, monthly, quarterly, semiannually

INFORMATION	DEFINITION	EXAMPLE/GUIDELINE
Data Elements	The data inputs to the performance measure formula; used to determine whether the current information systems are capable of generating the information required	e.g., number of employees exited; total number of employees
Data Source	The source of the information for each data element (i.e., where that information is captured and maintained)	e.g., staff evaluation report; external stakeholder outcomes
Reporting Format	Method of communicating the results of the performance indicator	e.g., a comparison of results over time, actual against target/plan, a comparison against same period last year, etc.
Owner	The person who will be held accountable for the performance results of the indicator	Should be the person who has decision-making authority over the elements of the performance measure
Benchmarking Opportunity	Document the peer organisation(s) that currently use the performance measure, where applicable	List of peer organisation(s) utilising the same performance measure

KPI Implementation

The KPI does not implement itself no matter how sophisticated the tracking and reporting system might be. The idea behind KPIs is that organisations need to use them to identify areas where they can achieve breakthrough success and then follow this up by assigning relevant goals to employees. In some cases there is a direct relationship between the KPI name and the expected employee contribution. Take, for example, an organisation that has a KPI of increasing revenue growth by 10 percent. The associated KPI for an employee can be to increase revenue from allocated customers. The focus of the employee will be clear, and he will know how his revenue generation efforts are contributing to the overall objective and the higher-level measures.

Other KPIs do not have a direct relationship to the work an employee does and, therefore, have to be figured out carefully. For example, take an organisation that has a key result indicator of 5 percent increase in return on equity. The same language, definition and formula cannot be used to guide an employee on what he needs to do in order to achieve the overall objective. An organisation can, however, determine that one way of achieving this is to increase miscellaneous income and allocate a goal to the finance professional who is responsible for disposal of assets to ensure that he gets a good deal each time so as to contribute to the overall outcome. Another dimension that you need to figure out as a manager is the uniqueness of your organisation. A KPI of reducing administrative costs by 5 percent, for example, would be managed differently in a farm compared to a bank or insurance company. In this case the manager needs to identify the business-critical events in the department that relate to the overall KPI.

Business-Critical Events

Business-critical events (BCEs) are events that drive the company's overall performance and set the tone for how people think and behave. Business-critical events must be narrow enough that the desired behaviours required for it to achieve the business objective can be precisely defined. BCEs usually revolve around small groups whose behaviours have a disproportionately large impact on company performance and organisational culture. Organisations do not need to outperform competitors at everything they do to win in the marketplace. By focusing on business-critical events, organisations can become much more efficient and effective in where they spend their time and investment on performance improvement. Once these business-critical events have been identified, the manager can then trace them to the objective of revenue growth or cost reduction and assign a unique KPI for the individual or group of individuals who share in the performance of those events. You may also look at positive deviants in order to identify what it is that they do to perform better than others. Positive deviants are people who constantly meet their performance objectives such as due dates for projects and have a low rate of follow-up work needed. By examining the behaviour of positive deviants, you can come up with key performance indicators that underlie their performance.

KPI Reports

KPI information needs to be reported to the various stakeholders from the board, and from senior management to individual employees. The fact that KPI reports are even available on a daily basis means that management can tell how the month is going or what kind of performance they expect. This is useful because the time spent reviewing these reports can then be used to focus attention on areas that are causing concern or drive impetus in areas that are tracking well. Employees can also have access to information relating to the organisation's performance provided that this does not include business secrets or information that could be harmful if it lands in the hands of competitors. Some organisations share information on their financial performance, and when it's time for allocating bonuses and other rewards, employees tend to feel that their actions were not recognised and that the sharing of the information was meaningless to them on an individual level. They then tend to ignore similar information-sharing sessions in the future because of a feeling that they are not going to change how the cake gets shared. The chapter on rewards and recognition sheds more light on this dilemma of sharing information.

In summary, a key performance indicator (KPI) is a metric that shows the fiscal health of your business and can represent whether you are successfully running your business. It can show long-range trends year over year and be the target you aim for every day. KPIs can also inform you about the areas to focus training efforts on, as you will notice domains whose performance has not changed in the way you expected and uncover training gaps on further examination. The information you obtain about the health of your business will also help you in implementing your rewards management system or policy in an objective way since the information obtained is visible and accessible to all relevant stakeholders. Development, management and maintenance of KPIs is a discipline that needs to be understood and embraced throughout the organisation for it to provide truly outstanding performance results. Such a management activity is key to enhancing the objectivity and fairness in the distribution of performance rewards.

Case Study 8: Using Dashboards to Report on KPIs

There are many ways of tracking performance against KPIs, and one of these is the use of dashboards. A leading bank developed a dashboard in which it was able to track the performance of business banking on a weekly basis. The dashboard displayed key performance information and brought issues to the attention of management. The bank tracked the following key performance indicators: the bank's earnings in relation to all of the resources it has at its disposal; how much profit it generates with the money shareholders have invested; profitability; personnel-related expense and operational efficiency; occupancy expenses in relation to operating expenses; operational efficiency in relating to accounting; and problems in the loan portfolio.

Well-designed dashboards enable better and faster decision-making. In fact, surveys have shown that two of the key benefits of implementing dashboards are faster decision-making and reduced administrative work in research and analysis.

To succeed with dashboards you need to:

- Develop a model of your business process. Define the causal links in that process.
- Define key performance indicators using management science methods, such as those of Lean Six Sigma.
- Be willing to change your business model and causal links if changes to a driver do not create change in the objective.
- Collect the data for "right-time" decisions—surveys have shown that the average enterprise-level dashboard system uses six to seven data sources.

- Tailor dashboards to the needs, data sources and decision factors facing individuals.
- Build a scalable system able to expand to meet the needs of the organisation.
- Absorb fact-based management and the use of dashboards into daily operations.

Dashboards are used at the tactical and operational level. Managers use dashboards to monitor the success of tactical initiatives, such as marketing campaigns or sales performance during a specific new product introduction. Managers and supervisors use dashboards to monitor operational performance on a weekly, daily, and even hourly frequency. Operational uses include areas such as monitoring manufacturing quality or budget variance on projects.

Executives use scorecards to monitor strategic alignment and success with strategic objectives, and the balanced scorecard is undoubtedly the best-known corporate strategy scorecard, used to help organisations align with strategy. Other forms of executive scorecards can show multiple dashboards that give an executive-level view into operational or functional performance.

Sample Process for Designing Key Performance Indicators

STEP	DESCRIPTION	EXAMPLE
Strategic Goal	Start the development of your KPI design with the associated strategic objective.	• Example 1: Increase customer satisfaction. • Example 2: Increase our profits.
Identify Audience and Access	Identify and name the audience for the indicator that you want to design and clarify who will have access rights to it.	• Example 1: The *Increase Customer Satisfaction* objective will be linked to the performance of the marketing department; therefore they and the board of directors will be the audience and have access to it.

STEP	DESCRIPTION	EXAMPLE
		• In a like manner the profit objective will be of interest to the board of directors and the finance department.
Key Performance Questions	Pose the key performance questions these indicators are helping to solve.	• To what extent are our customers satisfied with our service? • To what extent are we generating bottom-line results?
Use of the Indicator	Describe how the insights this indicator generates will be used and outline how this indicator will not be used.	• Example 1: The indicator will be used to assess and report on our customer success internally. It will not be used to assess performance of individuals or to determine bonus payments. • Example 2: The indicator will be used to assess and report financial performance internally and externally. It will also be a key indicator to determine executive pay.
Indicator Name	Pick a short and clear indicator name.	• Example 1: Net promoter score • Example 2: Net profit
Data Collection Method	Describe how the data will be collected.	• Example 1: The data will be collected using a customer web-based survey. • Example 2: The data for the net profit metric is collected from the income statement within the finance and accounting system.

STEP	DESCRIPTION	EXAMPLE
Assessment/ Formula/Scale	Describe how performance levels will be determined. This can be qualitative, in which case the assessment criteria need to be identified, or it can be numerical or use a scale, in which case the formula or scales with categories need to be identified.	• Example 1: Using a 0 –10 scale (*not at all likely* to *extremely likely*) participants answer: How likely are you to recommend us to a friend? NPS = % of Promoters (score 9 –10); Passives (score 7 or 8) and minus 5 detractors (score 0 –6) • Example 2: Net Profit ($) = Sales Revenue ($) minus Total Costs ($)
Targets and Performance Thresholds	Identify any targets, benchmarks and thresholds for traffic lighting.	• Example 1: 55% by the end of 2020 • Example 2: $1,250,000 by the end of 2020
Source of Data	Describe where the data will come from.	• Example 1: Survey of existing customers • Example 2: Finance and accounting system
Data Collection Frequency	Describe how frequently this indicator will be collected. If possible include a forward schedule.	• Example 1: Monthly data collection; sample 10% of our customer data base • Example 2: Weekly
Reporting Frequency	Outline how frequently this indicator will be reported to the different audiences (if applicable).	• Example 1: Monthly • Example 2: Weekly
Data Entry	Name the person or role responsible for collecting and updating the data.	• Example 1: Paul Patrick, marketing officer • Example 2: Peter Paul, finance officer

STEP	DESCRIPTION	EXAMPLE
Expiration/ Revision Date	Identify the data as long as this indicator is valid.	• Example 1: 24 months • Example 2: Target to be revised annually

KPI Costs, Completeness and Consequences

Once you have completed the design of the KPI using the steps outlined previously, you need to validate it on the basis of cost, completeness and possible unintended consequences. In relation to costs you need to estimate the costs incurred by introducing and maintaining the indicator. If the information is readily available, the costs will tend to be low or nonexistent. If you, however, have to launch a survey or implement an internal system you need to estimate the cost of doing so. The completeness of the indicator helps you to assess how well the indicator that you have developed will help answer the associated key performance questions. You should also identify possible limitations; for example, the indicator might be able to answer one aspect of a key performance question but not every aspect. A KPI can provide you with a figure or metric which might need to be supplemented with unstructured feedback about what is particularly good about the company's service offering and what could be improved. Other times it is important to review key performance indicators in relation to others so as not to pursue an objective while diluting another objective or compromising the complete view of the organisation's performance; for example, the net profit indicator is useful but you may want to complement it with other indicators such as revenue, profit margin, operating profit and return on assets so as to give a long-term view of performance. A KPI may at times have unintended consequences such as driving the wrong behaviour or individuals cheating on it. In a survey, for example, staff could influence customers to respond in a certain way, limiting the objectivity of the survey; or people might conceal results and reveal them only when an indicator gets measured, especially if the indicator is associated with bonuses or similar forms of rewards.

Management and executive teams should therefore be deliberate in which top key result indicators they will focus on in a given period and develop aligned performance indicators and key performance indicators using the 10/80/10 rule. These KPIs will drive performance in a substantial manner towards achievement of the stated goals. This will increase focus from all staff on the things that truly matter most, and it will ultimately provide a rational, objective, transparent and fair basis for the allocation of rewards and realigning staff efforts.

CHAPTER 8

ACTIVITIES TO REWARD AND RECOGNISE PERFORMANCE

"Recognition is a reward in itself. Any form of appreciation,
even a small word, is important."
—VIKRANT MASSEY

THE ACTIVITIES DIMENSION OF THE PERFORMANCE framework allows you to think and consider what other activities you should carry out. The performance management calendar is a collection of activities that the organisation intends to carry out over the performance period. The activities dimension is one that requires strengthening in many organisations because most activities that are planned within that calendar rarely take place, and if they do, they tend not to be carried out with the same rigour as others. Something that bears much repeating is the fact that performance management is a process and not an event. Performance calendars represent this processual nature of performance management; however, managers tend to view performance management as an event through which employee performance reviews are carried out at least once a year. Other activities such as communicating expectations, coaching and providing ongoing feedback tend largely to be ignored or stacked up very close to the performance appraisals with little evidence of the same during other times of the period of performance.

Smart Logistics, a leading player in the provision of security appliances and equipment, launched its operations in the Middle East. The company wanted to continue in its growth ambitions, and as part of its annual process it developed objectives and cascaded them to its different departments. The achievement of these objectives by the respective teams would lead to the achievement of the overall objectives of the company. The company therefore decided to introduce a team reward to any team that would achieve or exceed their goals. The company offered an expenses-paid holiday to the best performing team. One of these eligible team leaders introduced the idea to his team and excited them about it. They even developed a meeting routine, where every two weeks they would discuss the team's performance relative to the set targets up to that time. They would extrapolate their performance and say that if the trend continued they would be eligible for the unprecedented reward. By the end of the third quarter it became clear that the team would be in the running for this reward, as their financial and operational performance had been in line with or above the set targets. The only requirement was to keep the momentum over the fourth quarter. They managed to do this and achieve the unachievable. The team of seven in the fast-moving appliances section received the reward and went on a paid holiday as a team where they bonded and carried out different kinds of team activities while also enjoying the sights of a new country. The impact on team motivation was high; however, Smart Logistics did not continue the practice, and the team that had performed so well before started falling apart.

Incentives are promises of a reward. The promise is that good things will happen if people behave in certain ways, engage in specific activities and achieve certain results. Rewards are how organisations fulfill the promise. Recognition is how the organisation acknowledges and shows appreciation for people engaged in the desired behaviours and for the accomplishments that ensue. Awards are a type of recognition or reward that usually take the form of a certificate, a trophy or a cash bonus. Incentive plans and recognition plans are programs organisations put in place to manage what behaviours and results are rewarded and how. These programs usually specify the criteria for using incentives and how rewards are earned. An employee's salary is not considered as an incentive because in many organisations, people will get paid even when they don't put their best foot forward.

An incentive can be a promise of a future reward, such as a bonus based on some percentage of the organisation's earnings at the end of the fiscal year. It can also be something that is given to encourage the continuation of specific behaviours or activities, like a paid lunch if a project is on schedule. Recognition programs may use financial rewards like gift certificates or a company jacket, or nonfinancial awards like a personal or public thank-you, a memo in the personnel file, or a letter to upper management telling them about a person's work. Financial rewards—for example, money, trips, time off or large gifts—are susceptible to being treated as taxable income. The words "incentives," "recognition," "rewards" and "awards" are used interchangeably in everyday conversation. But however you use them, it is important to be clear about what you want to accomplish. The table below shows some of the differences.

FACTOR	INCENTIVE	REWARD
What it is	• A promise of a future reward • Something earned to encourage the continuation of or the achievement of specific results, behaviours or activities	• Something given after the fact in appreciation of good work or acknowledgment of some result or achievement • Something given to encourage the continuation of specific behaviours or activities
When it occurs	• Before, during or after an activity, event or result	• Either during an activity, after a result or after the fact
Purpose	• To encourage and motivate people to behave in specific ways or to achieve improved results • To provide direction	• To motivate when done during an activity • To acknowledge when done after the results are in

FACTOR	INCENTIVE	REWARD
Criteria	• Tied to desired results • May be tied to behaviours that lead to results	• Tied to desired results or specific behaviours that lead to results

Here are some of the mistakes managers and supervisors make when they want to motivate people or recognise their accomplishments:

- They fail to point out the importance of the work to be done.
- They discount the significance of a personal thank-you, general courtesies and politeness.
- They are unclear on their purpose—whether they want to encourage specific behaviours or reward results.
- They fail to link the reward or recognition to performance.
- They do not reward people fairly or equitably.
- They think treating everyone the same is best.
- They think treating everyone differently is best.
- They reward meaningless results.

There are many ways of recognising excellent or good behaviour in organisations, and these range from methods that have no cost to others that involve a financial outlay. The reason for performance outcomes that meet or exceed expectations is to ensure that the performance levels do not dip. From a performance management perspective, the first question you should ask yourself is what you want to accomplish by using incentives or rewards. What is the result you want? The second question to ask is how you will know whether the incentive or reward did what you wanted it to do. Performance improvement means following a systematic process to identify and use appropriate incentives to get the results you want.

Without a systematic process, you risk motivating the wrong behaviours and rewarding people whose work does not contribute to long-term success. If you fail to encourage the behaviours that lead to results and wait until the results come in to recognise what people accomplished, you risk not getting the outcomes you want. You must decide whether to use incentives to encourage the behaviours and activities you believe will achieve the results or to wait until the results come in and reward those people who were successful.

The list below provides some of the tools you can use to incentivise your staff:

1. Thank-you email or letter
2. Certificate
3. Photo displayed publicly
4. Spot cash
5. Box of chocolate
6. Gift cards
7. Coffee with the manager
8. Lunch with the boss
9. Meal voucher
10. Extra day off
11. Flexi-time
12. Gadget (iPad)
13. Shopping voucher
14. Company-branded merchandise
15. Paid holiday
16. Assignment to special projects
17. Secondment
18. Bonus
19. Vehicle
20. Incentive pay
21. Long-term incentive

The above list is not exhaustive but is provided to help managers consider the concept and options of the reward. Many managers feel helpless to define the type of rewards they can offer to their staff for work accomplishments. Starting with a list like this and armed with a number of performance scenarios, a manager through the support of his human resource business partner can launch a survey in which he consults his staff on what kinds of rewards they would like to receive after carrying out their work exceptionally. The survey would provide scenario-type questions, and even though they are not exhaustive, future reward decisions can be made on the basis of scenario similarity. A survey of this type is illustrated below. You can customise the survey in any way you wish so as to derive maximum benefits from it. By instilling predictability in the whole area of performance rewards, employees are clear on what they are working towards and the kind of recognition they will receive. A large multinational company in Europe decided to offer boxes of chocolate to all employees during the COVID-19 pandemic and was pleasantly surprised at how positively they were received. Each box of chocolate had a note from the company leadership telling the employee that he and his contribution to the company were valued, and even more so when he had to make sacrifices in order to achieve business results in the midst of a pandemic.

Identifying Effective Rewards

In order to best capture the minds and hearts of employees who are the recipients of rewards, I recommend that you carry out a survey to find out from employees what kind of rewards or forms of recognition would be most attractive to them. An example of such a survey is shown below.

EMPLOYEE REWARDS AND RECOGNITION SURVEY

The purpose of this survey is to find out what our employees value in terms of rewards and recognition.

For each question please select a single response unless the question requires more than one response. Your responses will help us align our rewards and recognition system to your preferences. Please feel free to add any more information in the space provided at the end of the survey.

Name: _____ Department: _____

Instructions: For each of the following situations please select the performance reward that you feel would be most meaningful to you.

1) While you were in the office you noticed a colleague carrying out an activity which, had you not reported it, would have resulted in the organisation losing $100,000. Your manager would like to reward you for going beyond the dictates of your job description. What reward would please you most?

☐ A gift voucher

☐ A spot cash award

☐ Time off

☐ A paid holiday

☐ A thank-you certificate

☐ Other. Please state: _____

2) You were assigned ten performance objectives for the year, and by the eighth month you have exceeded the expectations by over delivering on each of the objectives. Your manager would like to reward you for this level of performance. What reward would please you most?

☐ A gift voucher

☐ A spot cash award

☐ A cash bonus

☐ A paid holiday

☐ A thank-you certificate

☐ Other. Please state: _____

3) You are on a team of five, and one of your team members has been unwell for the last few days. This absence has resulted in some tasks being delayed, and there is an approaching deadline for submission of your most important team task. You manage to convince your team on alternative working arrangements including shortening your lunch breaks over the next week so as to cover up for the absent colleague. Using this approach you are able to complete the task to the satisfaction of all stakeholders. Your supervisor wants to reward you. What reward would show appreciation for your work the most?

☐ A box of chocolate

☐ A spot cash award

☐ Time off

☐ A paid holiday

☐ A team lunch

☐ Other. Please state: _____

4) You have noticed that one of the projects in the company is working on developing tools and processes for working with robots. Though you are in sales you volunteer to work on this project. Your sales targets remain the same and you manage to achieve them while contributing adequately to the robotics team. Your boss noticed that you took on the additional work on your own initiative and wants to reward you. What reward would you choose?

☐ Lunch with the boss

☐ A spot cash award

☐ Time off

☐ A gift voucher

☐ A thank-you certificate

☐ Other. Please state: _____

5) Your team has developed a balanced scorecard for the financial, customer, internal processes and learning and growth perspectives. The targets, actions and initiatives are assigned to different team members, and at the end of the performance period the team has met all stated objectives by over 120 percent as reported in the organisation's reporting system. Your boss and senior managers are very happy about your team's performance and ask you to select a reward from the list below. Which one would you choose?

☐ A cash bonus

☐ A spot cash award

☐ Time off

☐ A paid holiday

☐ Profit sharing

☐ Other. Please state: _____

6) The company carried out a survey of all its customer service agents, and most customers rated you top. You are entitled to a reward. Which of these will you choose?

☐ A gift voucher

☐ A spot cash award

☐ A framed photo of you at reception

☐ Coffee with your manager

☐ A thank-you certificate

☐ Other. Please state: _____

Additional comments:

_____

_____

_____

_____

_____

The results of such a survey can be used to develop a rewards framework that will guide managers in understanding which situations merit a reward and what kind of reward should be offered. Employees who receive such recognition should also be made known to the rest of the workforce so that everyone knows that the organisation is serious about performance and to eliminate miscommunication and rumours about how rewards are managed.

Thank-You Email

The thank-you email or letter is a good way to show appreciation to the people who help you as a manager succeed or who have made your work life enjoyable. When you send out these letters to your employees, it will also benefit you as the employees will feel encouraged to perform better after receiving that show of appreciation.

Employee-of-the-Month Certificate

The employee-of-the-month certificate helps to keep your employees happy, motivated and loyal. You can use this certificate to show appreciation for the work they do for you and the organisation. The employee-of-the-month certificate is not costly, yet it is impactful because employees always want to feel that they matter and that their managers are paying attention to the hard work they put in for the organisation or the department.

Displaying the photo of the employee of the month is another way of showing the employee that you appreciate their work. This public recognition is not only a morale booster to the employee but also reinforces the behaviours that the employee is being recognised for. When used properly, this cost-effective method of recognition goes a long way in improving organisational performance. It is a method commonly used by hotels and other tourist attractions; the employee who offers the best customer service as rated by guests and coworkers gets to have his photo displayed prominently for a month until the next employee is appointed. Sales-oriented organisations also use this method in addition to other forms of recognition.

Spot Cash Awards

Spot cash awards have been seen as a way of instant recognition of individuals who carry out something unexpected, brave, important or who go out of their way to achieve organisational objectives in a spectacular manner. The value of the actual amount of cash is not the issue, but the very act of backing your positive feedback with a cash award is what matters. When you use this method, make sure that you are not rewarding short-term actions, which could end up reducing focus on long-term results.

Box of Chocolate

A box of chocolate gives the feeling that Christmas has come early, and that's why employees love receiving one in recognition of their efforts. It is also a good way to acknowledge team performance by offering each team member a box of chocolate. The value of the chocolate should typically not be too cheap, nor should it be too expensive, but the box can be packaged in such a way that it has something extra. Some organisations go the extra mile by branding the chocolate using the company logo and colours, which makes for a true employee experience.

Gift Cards

The gift card works in a similar way to the box of chocolate in the sense that you are trying to give a meaningful gift to the employee. It might happen that the team you want to reward does not particularly like chocolate or that they have received chocolate boxes a number of times. A gift card provides an option to reward those employees while giving them the freedom to choose the gift they want. There are two kinds of gift cards: open-loop and closed-loop gift cards. An open-loop gift card can be considered as cash because it allows the employee to redeem it for anything he wants in any shop. A closed-loop card, in contrast, is intended to be redeemed at a specific store or for a specific experience. A good way of using such cards is to link them to the consumption of your customer's products. A bank could give staff a card that allows them to shop in a customer's grocery store, thus enhancing your business relationship.

Coffee with the Manager

Coffee with the manager is a relatively cost-effective and efficient way of recognising your staff. Coffee can be substituted with any other beverage, and it is the time that the employee spends with the manager that has the motivational effect. Unless the organisation has a culture in which employees and managers freely interact in different forums, this particular method makes the employee feel special. If the coffee house or the restaurant where the coffee is being taken is prestigious, then that adds an additional dimension of excitement and achievement on the part of the employee. Managers can capitalise on the coffee experience to coach the employee or even to discuss non-work-related things which further makes the employee feel that he is special and that he is considered as a whole person and not just an instrument of productivity.

Lunch with the Boss

Similar to coffee with the manager, the lunch with the boss reward works on the psychology of association and the pride of participating in an activity with the senior-most leader of the organisation. In large organisations, the effect of this is much more pronounced as individual employees can spend months or even years without direct and close contact with the overall company executive. Imagine how an employee in a field office would feel being invited to the corporate head office to have lunch with the chief executive officer in recognition of an accomplishment. It is right to say that this event will be the talk of the field office for a very long time and that it will encourage the employee to put in even more effort in his work.

Meal Vouchers

You may also decide to provide a meal voucher to an employee who accomplishes a special feat to dine in a specialty restaurant or hotel. The meal voucher is fully paid and would typically cover the full meal of the employee plus an invited guest. Options can be provided for the employee to donate the meal to a charity of his choice.

Shopping Vouchers

A shopping voucher acts in a similar way to the meal voucher, but this time the voucher is intended to be used in a grocery store where the employee typically shops. The voucher could be equivalent to a week's or month's groceries. Employees who value work–life balance and being perceived as an individual with multiple responsibilities will value this kind of reward. Just like the gift card, the shopping voucher can be tied to shopping at a customer's business and having the dual effect of reciprocating their business and rewarding an employee.

Day Off

Some employees who value time out of the office would prefer to get an extra day off that is not part of their annual leave entitlement. The employee can select a day based on the workplace exigencies and use the day off as he pleases. I have witnessed that employees who have this form of reward tend to opt to use it on a day close to a bank holiday or a weekend so that they have more free days to use either for a short vacation, spending time with their family or even participating in an event or hobby. The employee returns to work fully energised and ready to achieve even greater feats. A number of employees value meaningful causes, and the accorded free time could be used to work at a not-for-profit organisation or carry out volunteer work.

Flexi-Time

Flexi-time as a method of recognition works in a similar way to time off. You should, however, be cautious in how you apply this because the COVID-19 pandemic made flexi-time and home-working an option available to all employees for health and safety reasons. Giving it to an employee in such an environment will not add much but will look like an avoidance of giving a true reward. If you opt to use it in a situation where it is commonly available to all employees irrespective of performance, then you should add something extra to it like not having to be in the office at peak time to avoid getting held up in traffic, allowing online attendance of departmental meetings or work-from-home Friday afternoons, or any other thing which you know the employee would like.

Gadgets

At times the best form of reward you can give to an employee who has achieved an exceptional result is a gadget. This could range from an external drive to a laptop, depending on the degree of achievement. Those individuals who like collecting things and showcasing their achievements will particularly welcome this form of reward. During town-hall meetings or end-of-year events, organisations can use these forums to recognise outstanding individuals and teams. Due to the nonperishable nature of such rewards, employees will also include the associated achievements in their personal profiles and CVs as it is possible to show them to an interested party. The award or reward can also have a letter explaining how the individual was selected to receive it, which gives it even more value in the eyes of the individual and of the other employees.

Some companies create branded packages of their own products or assorted marketing merchandise such as pens, folders, T-shirts, glasses and mugs, which they offer to employees. The good thing about this method of showing appreciation to your employees is that it is scalable, and the reward can include one or more of these branded items. In other cases companies such as those in manufacturing offer their own products as rewards to employees for their performance; this could entail a month's supply of bath products, cereal, flour and similar items.

Paid Holiday

Many of the previously discussed methods of reward and recognition are fairly cost effective. A paid holiday requires the company to pay for the travel, accommodation and other expenses for an exemplary employee or team. This means that the achievement being recognised should be quite substantial, and it normally is a financial achievement. In case the reward is offered to an individual, the individual is also allowed to bring a spouse or friend along. The paid holiday duration is usually short and would typically be a couple of days in a local or internal destination.

Assignment to Special Projects

Assignment to special projects is another way of recognising staff. There are many projects that organisations would like to carry out, but sometimes these get overlooked or even lose their urgency with the passage of time. One way of bringing these projects to life while at the same time recognising staff is to assign key staff members to them.

I witnessed a manufacturing company decide to place certain staff on a project and tell them that they were doing this in order to develop the employees' skills. The employees felt they were being sidelined because the project didn't seem linked to the future success of the company, and the way it was communicated to them made them feel inferior. In a bank, a number of high-performing staff were assigned to a project that sought to develop a new offering for the bank. The group of staff was highly motivated and delivered superior results. They even went on the organisation's fast track and rose into managerial positions within a short time. If you decide to use this as a method of recognising your staff, you need to make sure that the work being assigned is perceived to be of strategic importance and builds the skills of those involved. One way of doing that is to assign one of your key executives to oversee those assigned to the project to give it added importance.

Secondment is used by large organisations who have operations worldwide or across a large geographical expanse. High-performing employees are sent out on secondments of between six months and a year to a different office location where they learn different aspects of the business operations while being part of the new team. This experience proves valuable in terms of its ability to equip staff with multicultural skills, global exposure, experience and motivation. Being part of the few who get that opportunity not only increases staff motivation but also improves employer branding.

Bonuses

A bonus is a form of variable pay that can be used to influence employee performance or behaviour in order to meet preset objectives. Bonuses can also be used to reward past achievements or applied on an ad hoc basis. Both the employer and employee benefit from the administration of bonuses. For the employer there is ongoing motivation, capacity for maintaining pay competitiveness without inflating the annual wage bill, and flexibility to adjust the payments during financial downturns. The employee benefits by having more control over levels of remuneration, and higher payments are possible based on performance.

The payment of bonuses is usually linked to performance on an individual or collective basis, or company performance such as profits (or both). Bonuses can be categorized into four models. These are the distributed scorecard model, the funding and distribution model, the profit-sharing model and the individual scorecard model. You need to understand the advantages and disadvantages of each of these models in order to select and implement the one that works best for your organisation.

The simplest method of tying balanced scorecard performance to rewards is using the highest-level organisational scorecard as the barometer of success and arbiter for bonuses. Under this scenario a certain percentage of incentive compensation is available to employees if the organisation should achieve some or all of its goals. Each measure on the high-level scorecard is assigned a weight, with total weights across the four perspectives summing to 100 percent. Even though there is a tendency to assign the highest weight to financial indicators, their significance should not be so high and should not surpass other indicators. Profit-sharing bonuses are tied to the financial performance of the company and are typically paid out to all employees when the company reaches certain profit milestones.

For bonuses to be effective, they need to be set at a relatively high level to have an impact. However, companies need to practice caution by not setting extremely high levels that lead to undesired behaviours or outcomes. The calculation of a bonus should be simple. Employees should be capable of measuring their progress against targets and calculate themselves what payment level they may achieve. The bonus payment can be determined by using a formula or by setting a salary percentage or flat rate.

Vehicles

A vehicle is a type of reward that has been associated with organisations that are sales oriented and that have stretch targets. An individual will be eligible for this reward if he emerges as the best salesman in the company in a given year. Banks have also been known to use this method of reward for those individuals whose roles involve meeting the bank's target through stretch goals. Similar to a gadget, the employee will appreciate a letter that accompanies the vehicle explaining how they were selected for the reward. If a number of vehicles are offered, they could be of the same model or class to recognise similar high levels of performance, or they could be different models and classes based on the scale of performance. A higher and more recent model or vehicle class would be offered to the top performer, a lower model or class to the next performer, and so on till the available vehicles have all been issued out. Due to budget constraints not many organisations can use this method; however, it is good to evaluate it and see if there are performance scenarios that might merit its use.

Incentive Pay

Incentive pay is a form of variable pay, which is linked to the attainment of performance goals. There are a number of ways organisations can calculate incentive pay, including incentive pay as an additional amount to an employee's pay or incentive pay as part of an employee's pay which is withheld until targets are met. The latter method tends to act as a de-motivator in organisations which have implemented it, as employees feel that they are being subjected to a pay cut. Incentive pay as a top-up to one's salary has certain thresholds and performance requirements which when met determine the amount due to an employee. Some organisations compute incentive pay on a monthly basis and pay it on a quarterly basis.

Long-Term Incentive Plans

A *long-term incentive plan* (LTIP) is a company policy that rewards employees for reaching specific goals that lead to increased shareholder value. In a typical LTIP, the employee, usually an executive, must fulfill various conditions or requirements. A long-term incentive plan, while geared towards employees, is really a function of the business itself striving for long-term growth. When objectives in a company's growth plan match those of the company's LTIP, key employees know which performance factors to focus on to improve the business and earn more personal compensation. The incentive plan helps retain top talent in a highly competitive work environment as the business continues evolving in predetermined and potentially lucrative directions.

Aligning Rewards to Behaviour

Since incentives are meant to recognise and reward results, it is important to identify the right combination of results and the contributing behaviours. Alignment happens when the incentive plan gets people to behave in ways that lead to desired results. Therefore, the incentive plan should be congruent with the organisation's values and goals. If, for example, an organisation would like to incentivise safety promotion in the workplace, safety incentives would only work when the company combines them with the following:

- Clear expectations about all the factors that contribute to performance, including protecting the environment, doing quality work, controlling costs and providing good customer service

- Good documentation

The challenge is maintaining a balance across safety, environment, quality, cost and customer service. Other types of incentive schemes will achieve the desired results when the balance is achieved across customer, stakeholder, cost, quality and their ability to enhance employee experience.

Organisations also need to be careful about how they communicate rewards. If a manager, for example, offers a reward to an employee for going beyond his call of duty to collect a long-term outstanding debt, the organisation needs to make it clear that it is not encouraging employees to ignore immediate debt collection so that they can be eligible for rewards when the debt has gone uncollected for a period of time. In the same way the frequent reporting of performance results that organisations carry out these days should be linked or de-linked to rewards depending on the intent of the organisation. In the mind of the employee, whenever an organisation communicates excellent periodic performance, the employee believes that this means that the size of their award, usually a bonus, will increase. When this does not happen, it has a negative effect on morale and productivity. Failure to communicate periodic performance, by contrast, also creates a culture in which employees think that the organisation is not willing to share in the success through rewards. Striking a balance between disclosure and secrecy is therefore an important consideration for all organisations. Organisations should also consider the legal implications of denying contractually agreed rewards to individuals who have met the defined performance thresholds simply because the wider organisation might not have achieved its planned level of performance.

Case Study 9: Using Virtual Bouquets to Promote Team Goals

I introduced the concept of virtual bouquets to one of my teams as a way of fostering team cohesion and making each individual team member accountable and responsible for the development of fellow team members. Every week during the team meeting, we would have an agenda item during which a team member would nominate another team member to receive a bouquet. In doing so, the nominating team member would say what the other team member had done in order to deserve the bouquet. A team member would, for example, say, "I would like to give a bouquet to so-and-so for helping me to compile the report as I handled some urgent administrative tasks." The receiving team member would be very happy to be acknowledged in public and more often than not would smile, and I knew that such supportive behaviour would be continued and emulated by other team members.

As team members got to realise the motivational impact these virtual bouquets were having, the quality of the recognition got even better, and the team performance increased dramatically.

Managers and executives are responsible for developing their own unique reward-and-recognition mechanisms that promote the performance and well-being of their team members. To do this managers need to understand their team members very well and develop mini-schemes that work in their own setting. A scheme that works well for marketing personnel might not have the same effect when used in the fleet management section.

CHAPTER 9

NUANCES OF A HIGH-PERFORMANCE CULTURE

"The ability to change constantly and effectively is made easier by high-level continuity."
—Michael Porter, Author of Competitive Strategy

There are unique elements within organisations that call for changes or flexibility in the performance management systems. These include changes in leadership, mergers and acquisitions, the maturity of the organisation in terms of using various management and control systems and the workforce composition. Because these are specific to each organisation I refer to them as nuances. A *nuance* is a difference or distinction that affects the composition or packaging of performance management elements in an organisation.

For most people performance management is about goal setting and appraisals. A high-performance culture is a set of behaviours and norms that leads an organisation to achieve superior results. The way different organisations achieve high-performance cultures may differ; however, there are a number of essential elements that cannot be ignored.

The American research and advisory firm Gartner defines a high-performance culture as "a physical or virtual environment designed to make workers as effective as possible in supporting business goals and providing value."

Leadership and Performance Culture

A high-performance culture helps an organisation achieve high levels of performance and results consistently over time. Because it is a culture, the activities and processes described in this book cannot be taken as events and carried out one time. They have to be made to stick and be part of the organisation's essence. Building a high-performance culture should therefore be your goal irrespective of whether your focus is on your team, a department or the entire organisation. A high-performance culture can mean the difference between stagnation and growth, competitiveness and being left behind. Whether you operate in a nonprofit organisation or a business, your organisation will benefit greatly by putting in place the ingredients required for a high-performing culture.

Every author who has written on organisational culture has invariably mentioned the importance of leadership. Leadership is the foundation upon which high-performing organisations and groups are formed. Leaders set the tone, communicate goals, and directly impact employee performance in a variety of ways. In a high-performance work culture, leaders develop and interpret strategy, drive goal execution and are a catalyst for team performance. Leaders set the bar for performance through their behaviours and actions. They also exhibit enthusiasm for the accomplishment of challenging goals and demonstrate how to overcome hurdles that can get in the way of team execution. For example, a leader who works hard to exceed sales goals or learn a new process will inspire their employees to do the same.

Leaders of high-performance teams motivate employees and inspire them to give their best to the projects at hand. They are both cheerleader and coach, creating an environment where employees feel engaged and inspired. In setting goals and giving feedback, leaders in a high-performance culture communicate clear, measurable, and action-oriented goals. They communicate with empathy and give feedback that builds trust and encourages employees to perform to their potential.

Empowered and engaged employees support their leaders in shaping the vision and delivering outcomes that are in line with the organisation's strategic intent. High-performance cultures consist of individuals who possess the ability to make key decisions and own those decisions, leading to increased engagement. Employees who feel empowered to take action when a problem or opportunity arises exhibit increased engagement levels. Organisations with a high-performance culture do more than say they want employees to be empowered; they ensure that employees have the necessary skills and knowledge to use good judgment when making decisions.

High-performance cultures feature two-way feedback mechanisms, training that promotes idea generation and leadership that encourages employees to take ownership in the everyday performance of their roles. The element of allowing employee ownership of everyday performance is based on a leader's ability to trust his employees.

Continuous Learning and Development

A focus on continuous learning and employee development is a key characteristic of high-performing organisations. High-performance organisations recognise that people need to focus on continually upgrading their skills and knowledge to sustain long-term performance. Instead of occasionally introducing off-the-shelf training, they evaluate employee development needs and identify clear pathways for ongoing growth and learning.

Employee development in a high-performance culture also focuses on building the leadership pipeline and creating a deep bench of leadership capability that will fuel the organisation for years of growth. Leadership development harnesses the talent and passion of high-potential employees and ensures the sustainability of a high-performance culture.

Openness to Change

A high-performance culture is open to change. Like all organisations, those with a high-performance culture are not immune to the constant pace of change that exists in every industry. However, individuals in high-performance cultures approach change as an opportunity, rather than just an obstacle to be overcome. Organisations with a high-performance culture aren't afraid to rethink their strategy or reinvent jobs, work practices or other internal processes to achieve results. They plan for and embrace change and leverage it to spur innovation.

The characteristics of a high-performance culture give many cues about the behaviours and mindset of the individuals within that culture. If you recognise there are characteristics of your company culture that differ from that of a high-performance culture, it is possible to develop and execute a plan that will transform your culture and help employees adjust their behaviours in support of sustainable, high levels of performance.

Safety and Security

A high-performance culture is characterised by a sense of safety and security by employees. This not only refers to the physical security or safety but also to the ability of the organisation to cater to the professional, social and emotional needs of its staff.

Not every individual who applies to work in a given organisation is suited for the role. In fact, a high-performance culture requires that managers and leaders exercise selective hiring. The inclusion of team members into the organisation should not only be on merit but on the complementary role that those hired will play. One needs to look beyond the so-called hard skills and focus on the social skills that will allow one to integrate fully and quickly into the team. An individual might be a high performer or a high achiever in another organisation, but if you feel that the individual lacks the complementary skills to work in your organisation you should not feel obliged to hire them.

An offshoot of working in an organisation where you trust your employees is that you will promote decentralized decision-making. Imagine how much easier it would be to serve your customers if every difficult decision did not have to be forwarded to you as the manager or even higher up the organisational hierarchy. Employees would feel more in control of their jobs, resulting in increased job satisfaction. This would in turn produce better performance results in all other associated areas. Organisations that succeed in the modern economy ask employees to stretch to achieve challenging goals, demonstrate the discipline to meet performance demands, show a willingness to support and assist team members in accomplishing assignments, and earn the trust of others by demonstrating their commitment to the long-term welfare of the organisation and its members.

In the chapter on rewards and recognition we discussed the different types of rewards and incentives that you can include in your portfolio as a manager or as an organisation. This is a key element of high-performing cultures. The compensation that is offered in high-performance culture is high and results based. Indeed, there are many high-performing organisations which offer long-term incentive schemes that not only provide the incumbents with funds to undertake major investments but also commit the individual to the long-term results in a singular and focused manner. A large tobacco company offers its senior staff shares or stock at a discount. The executive holds onto the stocks during his employment and is able to dispose of them only after a given time, usually if he leaves employment. The share value rises based on the business performance, and the executives are vested in the long-term performance of the company because they have a stake in it.

Accelerated Training

The concept of training on steroids is one used to denote the nonstop nature of high impact and on-demand training. High-performance cultures develop and implement timely training solutions and interventions in the workplace for individuals and groups. This means that remedial action is taken immediately, and the areas that require improvement are addressed as soon as possible when they arise. It is like taking a car to the garage for regular service instead of waiting until it has broken down.

There is usually a status blur between leaders and followers in a high-performing organisation for a number of reasons. One of the chief reasons is that, in carrying out a task, a leader by designation might not be best suited for it at a given time and within given circumstances. A team member might be able to rally his fellow team members around a cause or an issue much better than the leader would. Another reason for this status blur is that in today's world leaders hire people who are much more qualified than themselves. This moves power to the team members, who are able to carry out the technical tasks required of them without necessarily having to seek guidance from the team leader. All these things result in reduced status barriers.

In the traditional economy, having information distinguished those who wielded power from those who did not. In the knowledge economy, however, information sharing is power. The information and perspectives different individuals have about a problem or an issue when clearly elucidated allow for the creation of better solutions and increased stake by team members in the outcomes of the decisions made.

Organisations that effectively incorporate the features of high-performing cultures tend to be happier organisations that have a distinct focus on their purpose and customers. These features cannot be applied piecemeal or selectively, as they work together just as the ingredients of a cake to ensure that the final product is not only appealing to the eye but also tastes great. Organisations should seek to establish a culture of high commitment, high trust and high performance.

Ultimately, the top management team and leadership at the top are responsible for creating an aligned and committed corporate culture that is essential to creating a high-performing organisation. A growing body of evidence suggests that organisational leaders who adopt aligned High Performance Work Systems are rewarded with employees who are more committed to their organisations and more willing to engage in the extra role behaviours that are key to organisation profitability and competitive advantage. Those who lead great organisations must understand the complexities that are critical to success in the modern organisation, be committed to values that resonate with employees, and embody those values in their own lives.

These practices are also relevant to small and medium-sized organisations, as well as the not-for-profit sector. The culture-wide integration of values starts from leadership living according to the organisation's purpose and ensuring that their own behaviours echo the values of the organisation. They then lead by doing and demonstrating that the results are attainable.

This breeds trust and commitment from the staff who then feel empowered to do more and to be more. Companies and their leaders who fail to incorporate superior performance management practices are likely to find themselves in a competitive position that rapidly deteriorates in the modern, fast-moving economy, ultimately going out of business as they fail to keep up with an ever-changing world.

CHAPTER 10

CONVENIENCE OF THE PERFORMANCE PROCESS

THE ELEMENTS DESCRIBED IN THIS book thus far require some form of documentation. This includes performance agreements, goal-setting forms, performance appraisal forms, performance improvement forms, performance dialogue guides and many others. These different tools serve the purpose of formalizing the performance management process. It is extremely critical in a large organisation because if the process is left to individual whim, a number of elements will be easily ignored and there will be subjectivity. The requirement or need for documentation must be matched with convenience and use. The rise in performance management systems of all types is a response to the need for maintaining performance evidence and documentation as well as eliminating the need for manual recall of key incidences and contributions of an employee over the performance period.

Understanding

Understanding your employees and understanding oneself is the beginning of enhancing convenience in the performance management process. All employees are different and bring different backgrounds, perspectives, insights, styles and preferences to the workplace. It is important for the manager to understand how these perspectives affect the employees' uptake of performance management information and how they consume the same. The manager should go further to understand the working styles and preferences of the different employees so as to tailor the different elements of the performance management process for each one. This tailoring might include altering the timings for performance discussions, the methods of giving feedback, the approach to workplace coaching or even the goal-setting process itself.

Ease

The second thing that gives rise to convenience is ease of use. The simplicity with which the performance instruments are applied and used is very important. The number of goals that an employee should be responsible for during a performance period should by and large be limited to between six and eight, or less if the employee is not in a supervisory position. In discussing performance goals with an employee, there are two considerations that a supervisor needs to make: Are the goals being discussed part of routine work, and are the goals being discussed going to make the employee a better worker or contributor? If the goals being discussed are part of the routine nature of work, such as attending routine meetings, site visits or customer meetings, the supervisor should dig deeper to find out what the intention of the meeting is, what the desired outcome is and how the outcome contributes to the achievement of business objectives. That outcome then becomes the focus of the meetings and allows the employee to not only report that he carried out a certain number of meetings but that he used the meetings as a means of achieving a given objective. If on the other hand the goal being discussed is part of the employee's personal development plan, then this should be linked to the organisational objective so that as the employee becomes a better negotiator in line with his personal development plan, he also successfully negotiates favourable payment terms for the company. This linking of organisational benefits to employee needs creates convenience by simplifying the focus from two elements to a single one.

Simplicity

The third characteristic that allows for convenience in the use of system tools and processes is the simplicity of tools. A number of features contribute to the simplicity. The first of these is the language used. The diction and terminology used in a performance management system should mirror the language used in the organisation. Sometimes a system may fall into disuse simply because it does not describe organisational elements the same way the organisation views them. Some systems, for example, have a feature referred to as a *goal plan*. This is the facility that allows one to set their goals for a given period. Some organisations refer to this as the *performance contract*. This lack of alignment in terminology might cause an inconvenience and users might prefer to use alternative methods.

The second way of simplifying a performance management system is to automate it. A number of organisations that use manual forms find that the compliance levels to the performance management system are low compared to similar organisations which have automated the system. This, however, does not mean automation at all costs. If the costs of automating outweigh the benefits, then the organisation might be better served by having a simple manual format that is easy to analyse and use. Paper-based performance management systems can be a challenge if a large number of employees are concerned. This makes it fairly inconvenient to provide the required attention and rigour to the process due to the amount of time filling in forms and the back and forth that this might require when handling multiple sources of feedback. The other aspect that is jeopardised is the limited confidentiality of the employee details as the paperwork exchanges hands across multiple individuals and offices.

Accessibility

Accessibility is the fourth characteristic that makes a performance management system, framework or tool convenient to use. Many systems in the market such as SAP's SuccessFactors require the designated person to release forms during the performance contracting and performance appraisal process. This means that departments that might be ready to carry out the respective tasks have to wait for the designated person to release the forms. This somehow compromises accessibility and may occasion a delay which has a rollover effect because when the forms are finally released the departments or individuals that were initially ready might be busier and hence further delay the process. This accessibility can either be addressed by user departments or individuals being able to trigger the release of the forms, provided that this is not in violation of the policy or prescribed calendar; even better, the system can be configured in such a way that it auto-releases the forms and communicates such release to the employees to commence carrying out their self-evaluations. Such an auto-release will not only increase convenience but will also represent a respect of the business cycle by allowing people to focus on the respective performance management elements when their workload demands emanating from external events have been reduced.

Continuous Feedback

Support for continuous feedback is another convenient feature or capability of performance management systems. This is a feature that allows one to enter feedback, performance evidence, observations and similar things as and when they are observed or as they occur in real time. This feature is further enhanced by the ability to enter such performance evidence in a variety of ways including text, images, sounds and video clips. This will allow the user who has captured such information to consolidate it when the evaluation, appraisal or feedback period arrives and present it to the respective recipient in a wholistic, unbiased manner.

Performance management is one of the key management systems that affect employee experience and thus has to be personalised as much as possible in order to improve employee experience.

Continuous Improvement

Convenience also requires continuous improvement because as the employee's tastes and preferences evolve and change so does the performance management system and its process. This does not mean diluting the effectiveness of the system but continuously reinventing and reimaging system effectiveness through the addition of features that improve employee experience or the elimination of features that do not promote employee experience. To be able to achieve this, organisations and managers need to be open to feedback from employees relating to areas of improvement. There should be ongoing discussions about what is working and what is not and how the different features and functionalities are affecting usability.

In the design of performance management systems, the phrase "one size fits all" is rarely used because an effectively designed system is one which not only caters to the majority needs through the standardization of key elements but one which customises the system components based on the individual requirements of key talent segments or in line with business imperatives and employee requirements. This ability to straddle the standardization-variable continuum creates convenience in the use of the performance management system and results in increased uptake by employees, managers and executives.

CHAPTER 11

ENVIRONMENT VARIABLES IN THE PERFORMANCE PROCESS

"Change will not come if we wait for some other person or some other time. We are the ones we've been waiting for. We are the change that we seek."
—BARACK OBAMA, Former President of the United States of America

PERFORMANCE MANAGEMENT, JUST LIKE ANY other business variable, is not static and is greatly influenced by the external environment. The attribution effect happens when employees blame negative results on aspects outside their control, while they attribute positive results to their own efforts. The existence of regulation and flux in the economy means that the performance management system will be affected by the fact that it is linked to the organisational strategy and to the strategy responses to the changes in environment.

The environment dimension also requires that performance is linked to changes in the environment. This situation arises due to the limited ability an organisation has to alter the environment in its favour.

Economic conditions are always changing, and these in turn affect the business results and performance of companies. An employee who has a performance goal of selling a number of units of a product to a prescribed audience may find that the demand for the product has gone down recently due to the available disposable income or other economic forces. The conversation that a manager needs to have with such an employee is to find out the degree of freedom with which he can alter the product variables in order to make them more attractive to the market or alternative segments that he may target in order to meet his sales target. Should any of these options not be viable after having been tried, the manager can follow a process to adjust the targets in response to the change in the external environment.

Demographics also have an external impact on the strategy against which the performance goals and targets are set. The income levels and the education levels of the target population have a direct impact on goal achievement. These demographics too can change, and the organisation therefore needs to be constantly studying its environment in order to notice a key shift that might create future business opportunities or even require a change in the company's products or services. The performance management systems should therefore be altered when such changes occur.

Competitive forces have a way of ruining a great performance plan. The company always needs to be on the lookout for competitive moves that might have an impact on its own performance. These include competitor launches of new products, price adjustments and altering some or more of the other product characteristics. A company's financial performance, for example, is a function of the moves it makes in the market to earn its revenue and meet its financing obligations. The methods competitors use to reward their top performers should also be studied, as employees are always searching for better opportunities. Studying what the competitors are doing does not always mean that one has to match them, but one needs to understand their competitor's actions and possible impacts so as to develop strategies and action plans to counteract the negative effect of those actions. The action plans and associated objectives are tied to the performance management system which then must be updated to include these additional variables. It may not be wise to wait until the end of the year or the performance period in order to make these changes, but some call for immediate response and adjustment of the parameters within the performance management system.

Government regulations come in various forms. These include local laws, regulations and taxes. Compliance to government laws is nonnegotiable. Businesses need to adjust their operations in line with government requirements. This adjustment must in turn be reflected in the strategy and in the performance management process.

Technology is a tool that is used for capturing performance information. It is also a tool for reporting on the various facets of performance. Viewed in this way, technology is a means of executing performance management tasks as well as a differentiator. The performance management process can be greatly enhanced by using technology. The technological forces that belie these advancements therefore need to be harnessed since they can alter the basis of competition in a given industry.

Social change happens continuously in today's world, and businesses study the impact of this change on their operations and on their strategy. The performance management process and its deliverables must also be configured to be in line with changing consumer preferences. One area in which this is becoming a priority is in the provision of timely and accurate feedback. Employees live in a world where instant gratification is the norm. They transfer these expectations to the workplace and expect their supervisors to adopt similar standards.

Stakeholder expectations are a key ingredient in the goal-setting process, as are customer expectations. The expectations of these groups may change during the year, and it is imperative for an organisation to assess the feedback and input that it receives from these key constituents in order to develop, measure and track these expectations and respond to them within the performance management system in the goal-setting or review process. An organisation ignores environmental variables at its own peril.

CONCLUSION

A T THE TIME OF WRITING this book the world had just gone through the COVID-19 pandemic, and many organisations went through forced business transformation. A number of organisations had to retrench staff and send others on unpaid leave with the hope of returning back to normal in the near future. Many initiatives have been carried out to leverage the power of online business, and there is still more expected to come from this growing use of technology. The future of work and meaning of work is constantly being discussed and debated as the human person comes at the center of all organisational initiatives. These changes make it important for us to rethink our performance management systems and evaluate what value we are obtaining from them. Performance management itself is evolving with the shift to working from home and flexible working. The oversight and monitoring role of a manager needs to be redefined if businesses are going to continue to prosper. This book comes as a support to managers and organisations to refresh their thinking on the important link between strategy and individual performance.

Performance management is one of those managerial activities that a manager has to consciously apply himself to. One cannot imagine that things will work out by themselves. Managers continuously have to figure out what is working and what is not and take remedial measures. Performance improvement activities correspond to the nature of the human being who is wired to grow and continuously seek excellence. By supporting your staff in improving their performance, you are not only helping the organisation achieve its goals, but you are also supporting the employee in his dignity as a human person because there is not a single employee who cannot benefit with performance improvement support and development.

One might be tempted to imagine that the practice of performance management as described in this book would pose an additional burden to managers in their day-to-day tasks. Indeed, many managers find the task of giving performance feedback to be a difficult one based on a number of factors at organisational, manager and individual employee levels. The tasks described in this book require that a manager build in the practice of effective performance management in his daily routine so that it doesn't pose additional cognitive or practical challenges. There are a number of personal effectiveness tools, including diaries, journals and automated notepads, which can simplify this task. Managers need to set aside some time before the day's work to review the day's expectations and to apply the appropriate tool to their employees at the right time. If an employee is going to be joining your team on that day you can already start drawing up sample goals while planning for his induction process. If an employee is consistently demonstrating untoward behaviour towards clients or colleagues, you would be advised to give feedback and determine other possible interventions. You will do this for every situation you are going to face or have faced and thus take more control of the results by proactively managing them.

Your organisation should continually be examining the different elements of its performance management system using a framework such as that described in this book and assessing the extent to which the elements are working together. Any weaknesses in performance management elements should be strengthened because, as it is often said, a chain is only as strong as its weakest link. If your strategy goal-cascade process is not creating the alignment that you desire, then that particular aspect should be examined. In some cases you will find that the apparent weakness of a performance management element boils down to how it is communicated or even how that communication results in differences in implementation or in results management. You should therefore review the communication messages that are being presented and how these are being interpreted to ensure that what you intend is what you actually receive.

Once you have selected the ingredients of your performance management system, you need to make sure that those ingredients work together and that they are aligned to the performance management philosophy in order to achieve the strategic objectives. You will then develop employee goals and initiatives to track performance using both self-monitoring tools as well as manager-led tracking tools. These may be on technological platforms or in simple checklists and forms.

You will apply different elements to reward and recognise your staff on their achievements that support the attainment of organisational goals. This can be done on a shoestring budget or with bigger cash outlays, depending on what behaviours you want to reinforce. You don't have to wait for the end of the year or the end of the performance period to do this. In fact, you should even be using rewards in a proactive manner. This does not imply waste but rather looking out for individuals and accomplishments that merit reward and engaging with other managers and employees on outstanding achievements that they have noticed among your staff or teams. Make it a habit.

Allow your system to evolve and take into account the external and internal exigencies that might require a change or an adjustment in the parameters and features of your performance management framework, being careful that it meets the overall objectives of results orientation while respecting the unique and varied contributions of employees based on their ambitions, personalities, skills, interests and all other factors that affect performance.

It is my hope that the reader of this book will find something useful that he can apply in his business and also that universities and academics can undertake research to help organisations improve their performance management practices while at the same time validating the practices and case studies presented in this book. For those aspiring to management and supervisory positions, this book is a means of fast-tracking your career prospects by providing you with valuable insights that you can use to build your skills in the discipline of performance management, and in so doing create habits that will lead to career and professional success.

Now put down this book and get ready to get more things done the right way!

EMPLOYEE ENGAGEMENT CHEAT SHEET

Managers will use a set of guiding questions to discuss with their subordinates during their one-on-one meeting, at the beginning of the performance period and during each quarterly review. The goal is to understand their subordinate employees better in terms of their strengths and weaknesses; understand key challenges they face and aspirations that push them to strive towards their career objectives; and help them achieve organisational goals and their own goals, ultimately assisting them with the support they need.

The discussions questions:

- *What big-picture issues do you want to work towards?*

- *What behaviour do you believe best exemplifies our company core values?*

- *What one area would you like to grow in, and what area do you currently find most challenging?*

- *What are your key motivators?*

- *How do you prefer to receive constructive feedback?*

- *How do you prefer to deliver constructive feedback?*

- *In which area of work do you value autonomy the most?*

- *What behaviour or personality trait do you mostly attribute your success to?*

- *What do you foresee to be the major milestone in your career?*

- *What one professional achievement do you feel especially proud of?*

ABOUT THE AUTHOR

PAUL MBITHI IS A MANAGEMENT CONSULTANT WHO HELPS HIS CLIENTS excel in strategy execution and development of a culture of performance. He has vast experience in performance management, culture change and organisational transformation. He has worked with a number of clients in banking and financial services, manufacturing, government institutions, law firms, hotels, energy companies and shipping, as well as with international organisations. He has also worked as a faculty member of leading universities and enjoys lecturing and facilitating programs.

He is the founder of Captivite Consulting where he is responsible for strategy, business development and client account management. He holds an MBA in strategic management from the University of Nairobi, a bachelor of arts from Moi University, and a diploma and higher diploma of the Institute for the Management of Information Systems (IMIS-UK), both obtained from Strathmore University. He is an accredited Executive Coach from the Academy of Executive Coaching, UK. He frequently writes in the local newspapers on topical issues.

His working experience spans a number of countries including Tanzania, South Africa, Kenya, Uganda, Rwanda, Burundi and Ethiopia. In these countries he has provided consulting, coaching, mentoring and training services to a variety of organisations.

He is a member of the Institute for Human Resources Management and an associate of the Institute for the Management of Information Systems, and he speaks a number of languages including French and Spanish. He plays tennis in his free time.